RIOTOUSLY FUNNY STORIES OF NUPTIALS GONE AMOK

If you or someone you love has had hysterics at dress fittings or has broken out in a cold sweat at the thought of being the center of attention, *Wedding Nightmares* offers a restorative dose of laughter for frayed nerves and short tempers. Here are dozens of unbelievable but absolutely true stories collected by the editors of *BRIDE'S*—from the tale of the bride whose limo was hijacked by an armed robber to the groom's father who was captured on videotape stealing cash at the wedding reception. Now, in the safety of your own home, you can savor the high drama and comedy of what must surely be the greatest test of devotion—planning your wedding—and bask in the hope that these nightmares will not be yours.

BRIDE'S & Your New Home is the oldest, most widely read magazine for brides-to-be and their families. Since 1934, the editors of *BRIDE'S* have helped millions of couples enjoy beautiful, memorable weddings and, more recently, have asked readers and wedding planning professionals nationwide to share their stories of ceremonies, receptions, and honeymoons that went amiss. Now they bring you the best of the worst—a delightful compendium of wedding disasters.

Wedding Nightmares

♥ ♥ ♥

As Told to the Editors of
BRIDE'S *magazine*

ILLUSTRATED BY LESLEE LADDS

A PLUME BOOK

PLUME
Published by the Penguin Group
Penguin Books USA Inc., 375 Hudson Street,
New York, New York 10014, U.S.A.
Penguin Books Ltd, 27 Wrights Lane, London W8 5TZ, England
Penguin Books Australia Ltd, Ringwood, Victoria, Australia
Penguin Books Canada Ltd, 10 Alcorn Avenue,
Toronto, Ontario, Canada M4V 3B2
Penguin Books (N.Z.) Ltd, 182–190 Wairau Road,
Auckland 10, New Zealand

Penguin Books Ltd, Registered Offices: Harmondsworth, Middlesex, England

First published by Plume, an imprint of New American Library,
a division of Penguin Books USA Inc.

First Printing, January, 1993
10 9 8 7 6 5 4 3 2 1

Ⓟ REGISTERED TRADEMARK—MARCA REGISTRADA

LIBRARY OF CONGRESS CATALOGING-IN-PUBLICATION DATA:

Wedding nightmares / as told to the editors of Bride's magazine.
    p.   cm.
    ISBN 0-452-26768-4 (pbk.)
    1. Marriage—Humor.   I. Bride's (Condé Nast Publications, inc.)
PN6231.M3W4   1992
818'.540208—dc20   92-53565
                                                           CIP

Printed in the United States of America
Set in Goudy Old Style
Designed by Eve L. Kirch

Contents

Introduction

Ever since my beloved, but very nervous, brother-in-law (The Best Man) forgot the marriage license and our wedding was held up an hour and a half as he and my husband-to-be drove frantically through Manhattan rush-hour traffic to retrieve it, I have been fascinated by the concept of wedding nightmares.

Weddings *never* go off without a hitch. Yet some tales are told of people who *get* hitched with more than their share of travails and still manage to come up smiling.

Is it Murphy's Law (that if something can go wrong it will)? Or is this the first of many tests of a relationship that determines whether or not it is on a sound footing—and whether the partners have the humor and/or common sense to carry on in the face of (inevitable) problems.

The following pages cite some extraordinary events. Some are hilarious, some full of white-knuckle tension and incipient disaster. But all portray the human comedy in the full flower of its imperfection. You may find yourself here—but certainly you, your family, and your friends will laugh and identify with the outrageous true tales of adversity that can turn a day of celebration into a day of calamity.

The fun of this book is that it gives the reader perspective. You'll want to read the anecdotes to friends, and count your blessings if they don't apply to you.

And when you hear another wild wedding story, send it to *BRIDE'S* magazine for one of our future issues, because as long as there are weddings being performed on this earth, there will be . . . wedding nightmares.

Pleasant dreams.

Barbara Tober
Editor-in-Chief
BRIDE'S magazine

CHAPTER 1

Wake Me Up When It's Over

❤ ❤ ❤

So—let go of lists, duties, and all thoughts of things you've forgotten. Though you had to hurry beforehand, this is the time to slow down and enjoy the fruits of your efforts. . . . Your careful planning, well-thought-out decisions, and cooperative efforts have enabled you to put together a magnificent wedding celebration.

—From *BRIDE'S Shortcuts and Strategies for a Beautiful Wedding*

❤ ❤ ❤

Mortifying Moments

Love can be shameless. One of the male members of the wedding party spent the entire reception at a large concert hall in New York trying to pick up a bridesmaid from another wedding in the adjacent room.

Unfortunately, the male in question was the groom.

The bridesmaid, probably sensing something wasn't quite right (could it have been the freshly placed ring on his finger?), kept demurring. But the groom would not desist from his quest for her name and phone number. So determined was this newly wedded Lothario that at one point he excused himself and ran back to his own reception to cut his cake with his new bride—then returned to woo anew.

❤ ❤ ❤

It's called a *snowball wedding*: both the bride (Elaine) and the bridesmaids were dressed in white. The maid of honor, a very pregnant sister of the bride, was to precede Elaine down the aisle in Michigan. But as she started her approach, the musicians saw her white gown and began triumphantly to play the "Wedding March." More than a few eyebrows were raised on the groom's side of the family—especially by those who had never met the real bride.

❤ ❤ ❤

The California groom was in the military and re-quested to cut the cake with his dress sword. It was a swashbuckling idea—except that during the photo shoot prior to cutting the cake, the excitable young man kept brandishing his sword when he gestured with his hands. Fearful that he would decapitate his bride, the wedding consultant stepped in and sweetly but firmly relieved the groom of his weapon until it could be safely brandished against the cake.

❤ ❤ ❤

To cut down on wedding expenses, June had decided to hold the rehearsal dinner at her own home in Califor-nia. It was to be a large, formal dinner party, overseen by caterers, but the bride-to-be still couldn't help feeling jittery.

Since she had always found gardening to have a calm-ing effect, she spent the afternoon immersed in her flowers and vegetables. It worked: by the time the guests arrived, June was calm and smiling, the consummate gracious hostess.

It wasn't until the bride-to-be was getting ready for bed that night that she realized her elegant prewedding dinner had not gone completely as planned. As she began to undress, she realized that she was wearing her

WEDDING PORTRAIT
George Peppard Weds Fourth Bride

❤ ❤ ❤

When actor George Peppard, then 56, exchanged marriage vows with his fourth wife, actress and painter Alexis Adams, then 28, they each took some literary license with the phrasing. First George put some heavy emphasis on the "richer" part of the vow, "for richer or for poorer." Then, Alexis began her vows nervously with, "I, *George*, take you . . ." George immediately jumped in and interrupted his soon-to-be wife with the quip, "Not so fast. You're not wearing the pants in this family yet!"

gardening overalls—and that she had worn them the entire evening! The gardening had so relaxed her that she had forgotten to change—and her formally dressed guests had all been too polite (or too amused) to bring it to her attention.

❤ ❤ ❤

The reception in New York City was in full swing when the bandleader, a violinist, went over to the dais where the wedding party was seated. When he leaned over to ask the mother of the bride how she thought things were going, she said nothing, only looked at him in horror. He turned around and saw that while leaning over, he was stabbing the 25-year-old bride in the neck with his violin bow.

❤ ❤ ❤

The Virginia father of the bride couldn't help himself—it was his only daughter, after all! She looked so beautiful, and he was so proud of her. He sobbed—no, bawled—loudly, as he escorted her down the aisle.

One person, however, was untouched by the emotional display—the bride's mother. "Couldn't you have played louder," she demanded of the organist, "and drowned him out?"

❤ ❤ ❤

The Kentucky reception had just started at the elegant club when the bride, Jacquie, seated in a long raw-silk gown, felt uncomfortable. She stood to readjust the material, and the back of her bulky dress caught the edge of the small cushioned wooden fold-up chair. When Jacquie sat down again, the chair closed—and she tumbled ungracefully backward to the floor. The groom quickly pulled her up. The bride's face was beet-red, but she hoped that if she got up soon enough, no one would notice.

But all eyes were on the bride—including those of the

maître d'. With an excruciatingly obvious flourish, he insisted on replacing the bride's chair. All guests watched as he squeezed in a standard-sized chair at the head table so that she could seat herself—like a queen on her throne.

WEDDING PORTRAIT
Lauren Bacall Weds Humphrey Bogart

Malabar Farm in rural Ohio, home of two of Humphrey Bogart's friends, was to be the romantic setting for the May 21, 1945, wedding of the actor and Lauren Bacall.

While the bride was upstairs getting into her wedding dress, she suffered from a bad case of nerves, and found herself running to the bathroom every few minutes. No sooner had the first chords of the "Wedding March" sounded than she ducked in again.

After a few minutes of music, still no bride. Bogie called up the stairs to see what was going on. The response, shouted down the stairs for all the gathered guests to hear, was loud and clear: "She's in the can!"

They were such a perfectly matched couple that they were even the same height. For once, however, the match maybe shouldn't have been so perfect. At a key moment in their wedding ceremony in Pennsylvania, the groom was expected to lift the blushing bride's veil. But because of their evenness in height, the groom didn't have the few extra inches to give him the needed leverage to dramatically raise the veil and drape it behind the bride's head.

For what seemed like hours, he vainly strained on his tiptoes and wrestled with the yardage of illusion, while the bride's blush began to turn angry red. The bridal party started to giggle, and before all decorum was lost, the bride's father, who had just given her away, stepped forward. He lifted his daughter's veil, gave her a kiss, and having gone above and beyond the call of duty, took his seat in a front pew.

❤ ❤ ❤

The last-minute question asked of every bride is not, "Are you sure you want to go through with this?" but rather, "Do you have to go to the bathroom?"

Having answered yes, the bride and her matron-of-honor sister scrambled upstairs and into the ladies' room of the Chicago church. Upon finishing, the bride leaned over to pull up her assorted lingerie. But while she had somehow been able to push everything down, she found she couldn't pull anything back up. The boning in both her backless, strapless bra and her elaborately boned strapless wedding dress rendered her immobile. "It was like trying to bend your ankle in a ski boot," she recalls.

It was a humiliating moment for the 33-year-old independent career woman—and it would have been a terrifying one, as well, if she had been alone. But she wasn't. The bride waddled out of her stall and plaintively asked Big Sister to be of assistance.

"Well, I taught you how to walk," said the sister, struggling to return the bride's panties, panty hose, and girdle to their rightful position. "The least I can do is pull up your pants on your wedding day!"

❤ ❤ ❤

The Michigan bride had carefully specified to her caterer that the cheese table was to have sumptuous portions of Brie and cheddar. She did *not*, she stressed, want the cheese cut into chunks with toothpicks in them—that was too much like a business meeting.

When the guests began to help themselves, the bride's father called the wedding consultant over to the buffet. "Come here," he said, laughing, "I want to show you something." The consultant followed him to the beautifully arranged cheese table and saw the guests attempting to balance champagne glasses in one hand while tearing open individually plastic-wrapped packets of crackers with the other.

❤ ❤ ❤

It was one of those perfect society weddings in California. The linens were custom-made; Tiffany candelabra

WEDDING PORTRAIT
Prince Charles Weds Diana Spencer
Princess Margaret Weds Antony Armstrong-Jones

❤ ❤ ❤

Archbishop of Canterbury Robert Runcie was tolerant of Diana Spencer's slipup when she recited her vows to Prince Charles. Nervously repeating her marriage vows in front of millions at St. Paul's Cathedral in London on July 29, 1981, she reversed the order of her fiancé's many names, calling him Philip Charles Arthur George instead of Charles Philip Arthur George. Just minutes later, almost gallantly, he could be heard to also flub his lines slightly, omitting the word *worldly* from his promise to share all his worldly goods. Nevertheless, the ceremony proceeded without pause.

The officiant at Princess Margaret's wedding to Antony Armstrong-Jones was not so understanding. On May 6, 1960, Dr. Geoffrey Fisher, then Archbishop of Canterbury, allowed no one to stray from proper form. When the princess stumbled over her vows, he stopped and had her redo them.

adorned the tables. There was one waiter for every two guests serving assorted gourmet delicacies, including chilled vodka and beluga caviar.

Still, the bride was not satisfied. After the first course, the guests were agog when she loudly asked for some sugarless gum and a toothpick.

And in This Corner . . .

The wedding-planning months had been rocky—the mother of the bride and the mother of the groom did not get along.

Still, they had managed to be stiffly cordial to each other until they stood face-to-face at the buffet table during the Minnesota wedding. No one is sure what set them off, but the bride's mother reached out, grabbed the wig off the groom's mother's head, and tossed it into the punch bowl in the center of the table. The wig made such a big splash that all of the linens and much of the food had to be removed and replaced.

❤ ❤ ❤

The wedding was in California. The mother of the bride hired the band and instructed them to play only big-band swing music. After the cocktail hour, however, the bride came up to the bandleader with a request.

"We want to dance now," she said. "Could you please play something more contemporary?"

"No problem," said the bandleader, and launched the band into some skillful renditions of pop music. The bride's mother marched up to the bandstand, furious. "I thought I told you to play only swing music!" she raved.

"Yes," said the bandleader, "but your daughter asked us to play some contemporary numbers, as well."

"I don't care!" retorted the mother. "I'm paying for this and you'll play what I want!"

The band dutifully switched back to the older tunes. Immediately, all of the younger people left the dance floor. The bandleader looked down and saw the groom was standing in front of him. Would he please play a certain Top 40 song? It would mean so much to them.

The bandleader complied. Again the bride's mother stormed up to the musicians. "Why are you disobeying me?" she bellowed. "I specifically told you not to play new music!"

"I apologize," replied the bandleader, "but this song was specifically requested by the groom."

"I don't care!" shrieked the woman. "I hate him!"

❤ ❤ ❤

One New York wedding ended with the bride and groom shouting at each other over whose family had a right to the leftover buffet food. "Your father's an S.O.B.!" the groom screamed at the bride.

To calm things down, a bridesmaid asked to speak to the groom alone, outside of the banquet room. Instead, he found himself locked in the plush bridal room with the bride—and, in private, their amorous feelings soon overcame their rancor.

❤ ❤ ❤

Twenty-five single women lined up to catch the bouquet at a November wedding in a New York banquet hall. Among them were two former roommates of the bride, both seasoned flight attendants.

The minute the bouquet left the bride's hands, the pair became airborne—and knocked each other to the ground. The sought-after flowers fell to the floor, as well, and the women grappled with each other for them—no holds barred. The striking redhead eventually emerged victorious, but her slinky black dress was torn beyond its slit. The other fetching lass not only came up empty-handed, but also ripped the underarm seam of her emerald-green bridesmaid's gown.

"The guys loved every minute of it," recalls the bride. "They were hollering and high-fiving. You would have thought they were watching *Gorgeous Ladies of Wrestling!*"

❤ ❤ ❤

When the couple got married in a New York State catering hall, the wrong band showed up. The bride's quick-tempered brother threatened to kill the bandleader, and started to drag him away to make good on the promise.

The poor musician begged the catering-hall owner to call the police, but he refused. "The family hadn't paid me yet," explained the owner rationally. "So I took the brother aside and said, 'You've got it wrong. You're kill-ing the messenger. Kill the head of the company. Or, don't pay him. But right now, you're having a wedding and you need a band. Don't act moronic!' "

The lecture worked. The brother backed off, and the band played on.

♥ ♥ ♥

The day of his wedding, the groom found out that his bride-to-be had slept with one of his groomsmen a few months earlier. The ceremony proceeded without incident, but at the reception he confronted his new wife with the accusation. In a hallway right outside the reception ballroom, the newlyweds had a loud fight. Word of the argument and its cause spread like wildfire through the bridal party and guests.

How did things get patched up? The old-fashioned way—everyone got very, very drunk.

♥ ♥ ♥

At his April New York wedding, the groom spotted his older brother arguing with the bandleader in the middle of the country club's dining room. The dispute, he learned, concerned the band's payment; his brother had handed the bandleader a money order instead of paying the $1,000 in cash, as had been stipulated.

The groom told the bandleader that he was sorry that a mistake had been made, but a money order was all that the family had at that time. Determined to have cold, hard cash, the leader of the six-man swing band made a proposal: Why didn't the groom open the envelopes of gift money and use that cash as payment?

The groom refused. "I wasn't going to sit in a corner counting out money from the envelopes when my guests were having dinner," he explained.

The band accepted the money order, but hardly in a graceful manner. They repeatedly sent messengers to the wedding couple during dinner to ask if they could start playing, although they knew they had been told to wait until dinner was over. Then, they departed the party for good after their first break—ending the dancing on a definitively sour note.

A Toast to the Happy Couple

At a Florida country club, the best man rose to make his toast. The groom, it seems, had been quite a ladies' man when he was single, and he thought that some of the women in the room might still have the key to his apartment. If so, the best man requested, could the ladies please come forward and hand over the keys?

Sheepishly, a young woman in the crowd came up and handed a key to the best man, and another soon followed suit. Getting into the spirit, the bridesmaids began digging in their purses, each one coming up with a key, which they handed to the best man. Carrying the joke still further, a waitress put down her tray and gave the best man a key. As the party continued, all the other waitresses and the kitchen help also came forward, each bearing a key.

❤ ❤ ❤

The introductions at the California wedding had just been completed at the head table and the best man was giving a rousing toast to the newlyweds. Suddenly, the bride's father stood up and cleared his throat.

"Excuse me, excuse me," he said, tapping on his champagne glass with a knife. "I would like it to be known that I have no pretensions—and nothing to hide." With those words, and to the bride's horror, he reached up and pulled off his toupee.

The guests roared with laughter, the bride's father replaced his toupee crookedly and, grinning broadly, sat down.

❤ ❤ ❤

The third and final daughter had been married off in style at the hotel. After dancing with his daughter and watching her cut the cake, the father of the bride made a toast.

"Well, I've married off three daughters," he began expansively. The guests smiled and he turned to his wife. "Now," he announced, "I am leaving this bag of bones!"

He turned and strode out of the ballroom. Divorce papers were filed that week.

❤ ❤ ❤

Was it a Freudian slip? When Mark, the groom's 300-pound brother and best man, rose to make a toast to the happy couple at their wedding reception, he got confused. Instead of toasting Paul and Leslie, he slipped and toasted Paul and Ann, the groom's *first* wife. (To make matters even more awkward, the brother and parents of the groom's first wife had remained close to the groom and were present at the wedding.)

The bride's 175-pound brother loyally leaped to the

bride's defense and punched the best man. "I couldn't believe it," says Leslie. "My brother had never gone to bat for me before!"

The band broke into the theme song of *Rocky* as the two men continued to tussle, and the bride sobbed. Friends finally separated the two fighters and the reception proceeded.

❤ ❤ ❤

The guests were buzzing during the New York bride and groom's first dance. The wedding seemed to be going smoothly enough, but it was hardly the kind of ebullient event Italian-Americans are famous for. The bride didn't even seem all that happy, and look at her now, in her groom's arms—wasn't she awfully stiff and unemotional?

After the dance, the maid of honor proposed a toast to the future happiness of the bride and groom. Then, the bride, who had been fidgeting throughout her maid's speech, strode up to the DJ and grabbed the microphone out of his hands.

"I'd like to propose my own toast," she announced. "To my best friend, the maid of honor, and my ex-husband. I caught them in bed together the other night and I hope they have a happy life together!" With that she threw down the microphone and strode out of the room. Immediately the bride's two older brothers, both groomsmen, jumped on the groom. Some of the groom's friends ran to his defense and a reception-wide free-for-all worthy of a Wild West saloon broke out.

The bride's father quietly took aside the DJ, the bandleader, and the caterer, paid them the money owed, and informed them that their services would no longer be needed.

❤ ❤ ❤

All of the out-of-town guests were getting acquainted at the rehearsal dinner when the groom rose. Instead of a toast to his future bride, he announced that both parties had amicably decided to back out of the wedding.

"But, since you're all here," the groom added cheerfully, "we're going through with the reception and party anyway."

The next day, they were a perfect host and hostess at their party—the rare "bride and groom" who had gotten enough sleep, didn't miss their cocktail hour because of wedding photos, and had plenty of time to visit with family and friends.

Intoxicating Interludes

During the cold months of winter, the bride had fallen in love with the idea of a summer wedding on a yacht encircling Manhattan. But on the day of her ceremony and reception, she began to have second, if somewhat irrational thoughts.

They would be holding 175 guests hostage for four hours! They wouldn't be able to leave until the boat docked! The party *had* to be an absolute, unmitigated success. If it were a failure, no one would ever forgive her.

To calm herself down, the bride began drinking shots of straight vodka a few hours before the ceremony. Halfway through her trip down the aisle, the bride stopped, caught in an inebriated fog. The groom had to come back up the aisle to retrieve his bride.

The rocking motion of the boat did little to settle the bride's stomach, steady her gait, or unslur her speech. The bride's father had to hold her upright during their dance together. Even the groom's amusement waned when he had to catch his bride from falling backward after cutting the cake.

It wasn't until the next day that the bride felt like she was on solid ground. "My wedding was truly an unforgettable experience I'll never remember!" she says.

❤ ❤ ❤

The groom thought it would be great to invite all of his college fraternity brothers to his wedding in Texas. When more than fifty buddies arrived a day before the wedding, he was promptly whisked off to an all-night bachelor party. The "fun" ended at three a.m., however, when the groom, an infrequent drinker, was rushed to the hospital with alcohol poisoning.

His bride, two sets of parents, and thirty of the fifty frat brothers waited anxiously in the emergency room as the groom had his stomach pumped. Fourteen hours later, the still largely incoherent groom was released—just in time for the ceremony. Two groomsmen walked him down the aisle and held him up at the altar.

At the reception, the groom lasted only through the salad course. Then his head dropped onto his plate and he was taken home to bed.

This might have cramped an ordinary bride's style. But the bride danced with every man at the party, and then enjoyed a collective escort to the honeymoon suite, courtesy of all her guests.

❤ ❤ ❤

The bride forgot one important maxim about mixing drinks on her wedding day in New York. After swallowing her prescribed medication for stress headaches, she sipped some cheap champagne with her bridesmaids, then took a shot of peach schnapps for good luck.

Waiting in the church basement for her walk down the aisle, the bride began to feel light-headed. By the time she said her vows at the altar, the nausea was in full swing. During the candle-lighting ceremony, she vomited. The minister sped through the rest of the rituals, and the bride was dragged up the aisle by her new husband and laid to rest in back, in the basement, where she remained unconscious for an hour.

An ambulance arrived, but the bride insisted on going to the reception. She climbed into the limousine with her husband, promptly fell asleep, and snoozed away the next three hours in the parking lot of the country club.

❤ ❤ ❤

In the wee hours of a New York wedding, the bandleader was asked by a drunken bridegroom if he could sit in with the band. Since the request came from the groom, he didn't see how he could say no, and handed over his vintage 1964 Gibson guitar.

It wasn't as painful as the bandleader thought it would be. The groom was indeed a passable player, and at the end of the set, the bandleader cordially but firmly took back his beloved guitar and went to strap it on. The groom, swaying with gratitude and too much champagne, felt he hadn't thanked the bandleader enough for the privilege of playing with him. Intending to shake the musician's hand, he collided with him instead, and the guitar went flying, knocking a huge and very expensive hole in the sounding board.

"Now," says the sadder-but-wiser musician, "I won't even let God sit in."

❤ WEDDING FROM HELL No. 1 ❤

Cynthia had the kind of wedding that most women "dream" about—after eating a pastrami sandwich with a side of onion rings and watching *The Silence of the Lambs* alone before turning in.

A month before her wedding in New Jersey, Cynthia went for a fitting. But her beautiful dress was so tight she couldn't even get it over her hips. The owner of the bridal shop uncharitably insisted that Cynthia must have gained weight, and suggested separating the dress at the side seams and having the manufacturer send a new back, two sizes larger.

When Cynthia returned to the shop, the allegedly enlarged dress still did not fit. When she and her mother returned for a third fitting (just eight days before the wedding), they waited for more than an hour only to discover that no further alterations had been made on the dress. After a furious exchange between Cynthia's mother and the shop owner, Cynthia finally received a dress that would fit in time for her wedding.

About two weeks before the wedding, the owner of the limousine service with which Cynthia had reservations telephoned to say that his manager had made a mistake and all his cars were booked in another city that day. He gave the now-overwrought bride-to-be the number of a local car service.

On the day of Cynthia's wedding, the car service sent two limousines to her house. As one driver attempted to back into the driveway, he destroyed her father's newly landscaped lawn. When the driver said that it was his "first wedding," they forgave him somewhat and ignored his repeated mutterings, "Don't forget to help with the bride's train and remember the champagne!"

They arrived at the church in time to take photographs, but it wasn't until the proofs came in that Cynthia realized that what the limo driver had been trying to tell them was that he had some kind of strange bridal-train fetish. "He was in every photo," Cynthia recalls, "clutching the back of my train!"

Later, as bride and groom were walking down the aisle in the recession, they noticed several friends leaving the church with wire coat hangers in hand. The limousine driver had been so concerned with the bride's train that he had forgotten the automatic door locks and locked his keys in the limo!

The remaining limousine had to make several trips from the church to transport the entire wedding party for a photo session in the park. After forty-five minutes, the wedding party was ready to proceed to the reception, but neither limousine could be found—the unlocked limo had been driven back to headquarters to pick up a spare set of keys. The bride and groom hitched a ride with the photographer, and other cars were sent back to pick up the wedding party.

Amazingly, the reception seemed to proceed smoothly, although Cynthia did note the absence of the piano player hired to play during the cocktail hour. While awaiting the arrival of the dance band, the bride felt a tap on her shoulder and turned "to find before me a woman in a black leather jacket, pants, and hip boots, with hair of three different colors," accompanied by three teenagers in similar attire. The woman informed the bride that the band's van had broken down an hour's drive away and would arrive shortly.

Two hours later, the hotel sent up a disc jockey, whose entire collection of music consisted of the complete works of Frank Sinatra. A member of the wedding party offered his cassette of electronic funk recordings, but that didn't seem like an appropriate serenade for the bride and groom's first dance.

Cynthia was in despair. Then the band arrived—finally!—and began setting up. But it soon became clear that it was not the band the couple had hired. The punked-out girl and her alarming friends took the stage—they *were* the band, and had just been waiting for the backup instruments to arrive. Most people might think Cynthia would rather forget her wedding day. Not so. "Believe it or not," she said proudly, "the guests said it was the best wedding they had ever attended!"

CHAPTER 2

Something Borrowed, Something Blue

❤ ❤ ❤

Your dress sets the style of your wedding,
and everyone else is outfitted accordingly.
You may fall in love with a certain dress
and plan your wedding around it. It could
be regal satin, graced with a mantilla to the
floor—so stately it belongs at a very formal
wedding. Or it could be a wide-skirted cot-
ton banded in pastel, suggesting a semi-
formal occasion outdoors. . . . A spectacular
wedding ensemble fits together harmoni-
ously. When one element of your bridal attire is out of place, attention is drawn to
that detail and away from your total
appearance.

—From *BRIDE'S Book of Etiquette*

❤ ❤ ❤

Ring Riots

Patty was cleaning the bathroom of her California home, so she carefully wrapped her five-thousand-dollar engagement ring in tissue—and then zealously flushed it down the toilet.

A frantic summons brought four plumbing experts who told Patty that the chances of finding her ring were slim. They inspected the toilet with mirrors, dug up her front lawn to examine the pipes, and tore up the street in front of her house. As a last resort, they built a special dam in the sewer, and used a huge machine to flush water into it. Miraculously, the ring was trapped.

The bill for this Herculean effort? Only four hundred dollars. The plumbers apparently figured they had been adequately reimbursed in the champagne that the ecstatic bride had broken out as soon as the ring was back on her finger.

❤ ❤ ❤

The setting for Gail and Adam's wedding was idyllic—an outdoor amphitheater atop a Colorado mountain.

The weather was perfect. The bride was beautiful. Everything ran as smooth as silk—until the ring ceremony.

Much as she tried, Gail couldn't get the ring over Adam's knuckle. The ring simply did not fit.

"I can't get it on!" the bride whispered to her groom, hoping no one noticed. But the acoustics in the amphitheater were too good, and the news quickly traveled from the altar to all the seated guests.

From the smiles and amused murmurs spreading across the crowd, Gail realized their secret was out and burst into laughter. Their photographer quickly captured the incident in a series of photos that still make the couple smile whenever they look through their wedding album.

❤ ❤ ❤

Right before the wedding ceremony in a Washington, D.C., suburb was scheduled to begin, the wedding consultant asked Douglas, the groom, for the bride's ring. He confessed sheepishly that he had left it at the hotel—ten or fifteen miles away.

Without missing a beat, the consultant took off her own wedding ring and gave it to the best man to use during the ceremony. No one had bothered to fill in the bride, and her eyes nearly popped out of her head when she extended her hand and saw the wide band with a solitaire instead of her much smaller and simpler ring.

A friend retrieved the real ring after the ceremony, and it was safely on the bride's hand by the time the reception began.

❤ ❤ ❤

The best man kept reaching for the ring in his tuxedo pocket, just to be sure it would be ready at the all-important moment. He was taking it out for one last look before the ceremony, when the boat on which the bridal party and guests had gathered unexpectedly listed. The ring slipped from his hands, bounced onto the deck, and started to roll overboard.

Without pausing a second, he jumped over the side of the boat, caught it on its way down, and then plunged with it into the sea. His shoes squeaked during the ceremony, and his formal wear was damp, but the ring was saved!

❤ ❤ ❤

Gregg was the groom; his friends knew him as an easygoing, fun-loving guy. Li-Chin was his bride; she was a sweet and sincere girl who took ceremony and ritual very seriously. They were being married in a formal ceremony at an old church on a California hillside before a hundred guests.

It was time to exchange the rings. The minister turned to the maid of honor, who handed him the ring for the groom. Then he asked the best man for the bride's ring and was handed a small box. The minister suspected something was afoot—the best man had been smirking throughout the whole ceremony—and during a brief musical interlude the minister found out why. Inside the bride's box was a hideously garish plastic ring, a joke the best man intended to play on his best pal, the groom.

Knowing how much the proper bride cherished the solemnity of the occasion, the minister was certain she would fail to see the humor in being handed the cheap plastic ring in front of all her guests. As the bride gave the groom his wedding ring and the groom recited his vows, the minister turned to the best man, and with fire and brimstone in his eyes hissed, "*Give me the ring!*"

Taken aback, the best man reached into his pocket and sheepishly pulled out the right ring, which was duly presented to the bride.

❤ ❤ ❤

Tanya and Eli wanted to be very sensible when it came to picking out her engagement ring. The stone and the setting had to be purchased separately, they decided, to make sure they got exactly what they wanted. After scouring five floors of an Illinois jewelers' mall, they finally found the perfect diamond. A little more searching led them to a jeweler who could give them the perfect ring.

It was all so neat and tidy that Eli worried it lacked a little romance. What was needed was an element of surprise. After dropping Tanya off, he called the jeweler. "I want you to add an inscription to the setting," Eli said. "You and I."

"You and I?" the jeweler asked.

"You and I," said Eli. "It's the name of a Stevie Wonder song that was playing when we first met."

WEDDING PORTRAIT
Lucille Ball Weds Desi Arnaz

♥ ♥ ♥

The romance of Lucille Ball and Desi Arnaz was as wild and zany as their stage personalities. On the same day that Lucy told the press their careers were too demanding for them to marry, Desi decided that they should. In fact, he said he wasn't waiting; they would marry the next day, November 30, 1940. Certain that he could get a friend—a local judge in Greenwich, Connecticut—to waive the requisite five-day wait, Desi promised to be back in New York City to perform at the Roxy Movie Theater that same night.

In Greenwich the next morning, the couple discovered they had forgotten two essentials: a Wasserman test and a wedding ring. While Lucy and Desi rushed out for blood tests, Desi's agent and manager combed the town of Greenwich for a wedding ring. His frantic search ended with a ten-cent copper ring from the five-and-dime. Lucy and Desi used the ring during the ceremony and later had it coated in platinum.

Desi's close-to-the-wire timing didn't allow for delays. By the time the ceremony was over, even a police motorcycle escort didn't get them to the Roxy on time. Desi carried Lucy over the threshold of the dressing room and the show was announced. The restless crowd was more than forgiving when the couple took the stage and announced their happy news.

"You and I," the jeweler said once more. "Got it. See you in a week."

Seven days later, Eli picked up the ring and presented it to Tanya. She was terribly pleased, but of course she wasn't the least bit surprised—until Eli told her to read the inscription.

Tanya's eyes welled with tears as she looked inside of the ring. There, in tiny, elegant script, were the words, "I want to kiss you in the snow"—in French. She looked up in bewilderment at Eli. He was grinning broadly. Not wanting to admit that the inscription was a complete mystery to her, she racked her brain, trying to remember some moment in their long relationship that might explain its significance.

Finally, she had to admit to her fiancé that although it was very sweet, she hadn't the foggiest idea of what he meant by "I want to kiss you in the snow," in French or in English.

"*What?*" said Eli, grabbing the ring. An angry call was made to the jeweler, who apologized profusely. He had given Eli the wrong setting.

❤ ❤ ❤

The priest had just asked Eric, the best man at Mollie and Jack's wedding, for the bride's ring. As he handed it to the groom, it slipped, hit the floor, and rolled under one of the many, many folds of the wedding gown that were draped over the altar steps. The decorum of the moment prevented him from diving under her petticoats to retrieve it. The groom looked totally helpless. It was up to the bride.

Skirt in one hand, train in the other, she backed up one step at a time—with the whole wedding party in slow pursuit. Everyone laughed uproariously as they all lurched their way, backward, down the altar staircase. Suddenly, out from one of the folds rolled the gold band. The best man spotted it, scooped it up, and the solemn ceremony resumed.

❤ ❤ ❤

Gloria's bridesmaids wanted her to have a very special ring pillow she would always cherish. They lovingly hand-embroidered it with the couple's names and wedding date and festooned it with ribbons—including one cleverly designed to tie the rings to the pillow so that the young ring bearer wouldn't drop them. Incredibly touched by her bridesmaids' effort, Gloria insisted on carrying it herself in the limo to church. Just before the ceremony was due to begin, Gloria realized she had left the ring pillow and—more important, the rings—in the limo.

"Don't worry about it," said the maid of honor. "The limo went on to pick up your mother. She'll see the pillow and bring it to you immediately when she arrives."

Which made perfect sense. Except that Gloria's mother was having her own troubles. The poor woman was anxiously waiting on her doorstep for a limousine that was never to appear. The limo driver had forgotten about her entirely and gone on to another wedding!

Somehow, the mother of the bride hitched a ride to the church. But the tenderly crafted pillow never made it down the aisle, and the ceremony was performed with proxy rings.

Gown Grief

For her December wedding to Jeremy, Gail picked an elaborately pearled and beaded designer gown. It would go perfectly with the ornate surroundings of the exclusive California hotel at which the reception was to be held.

But as she moved to take her place at the head table, Gail began to hear a strange sound—like hundreds of tiny "plinks." Looking down, she found that the glittering beads adorning her gown were dropping one by one to the floor—and bouncing across the room.

The banquet manager scrounged up a tube of Super Glue, which saved the remaining beads. The following Monday, Gail marched back to the bridal shop and demanded a full refund. An allowance was negotiated.

❤ ❤ ❤

Susan didn't want to put any wrinkles in her friend's wedding day, so she took careful pains to iron her custom-made bridesmaid's dress. She started to steam the dress over the bathtub, but before she knew it, the dress had slipped off the hanger and fallen into the tub. She quickly rescued it, but too late: the dress wouldn't even fit a large Munchkin.

Susan immediately telephoned her local dry cleaner, who reassured her by saying that the shrinkage could be reversed. We'll be right over, they promised. So Susan sat down and waited. And waited. And waited.

When it became clear that no one was going to come in time, Susan and the other attendants steamed, stretched, and pulled at the dress until it was large enough for Susan to squeeze into.

❤ ❤ ❤

When Ginger and her bridesmaids went to pick up their dresses two days before the wedding, they found the bridal salon locked tight and all the lights out. Frantic pounding on the door finally brought the manager, who explained that the store had been shut down due to a dispute with the landlord. He would be unable to deliver any items that had not been paid in full.

There was more than eight hundred dollars outstanding on Ginger's wedding gown, and at least half the balance due on each of the six bridesmaids' dresses! The bride was in hysterics. Finally, an agreement was worked out.

The bridal party paid the balance in cash, and the shop owner delivered all of the dresses to the bride's home the next day.

❤ ❤ ❤

Like most brides-to-be, Eve was nervous. But the usual planning jitters were further exacerbated by the stress of a long commute—her wedding was to be held in a distant city in Texas. Every week she had to travel back and forth, attending to all the prewedding and party details.

She was back in the wedding city yet again for a dress fitting, the designer and his assistants buzzing around her, when her nose began to bleed violently. Nothing seemed to staunch the flow, and before she could be taken out of the dress, blood had covered the heavily beaded medallions of antique lace.

Poor frazzled Eve was practically in shock. So was the designer—but fortunately, not for long. He had the dress cut apart, cleaned, and reworked. On Eve's wedding day, no one could tell that a stitch had ever been out of place.

❤ ❤ ❤

Nancy's and Craig's mothers burned up the phone lines between their two states, trying to coordinate dresses for the Maryland wedding. After lengthy discussion, Craig's mother went to a local bridal salon and purchased a lovely pale-peach gown. It was a perfect match to the color scheme—and, as she discovered on the wedding day, to Nancy's mother as well, who had bought the very same dress at a salon in her hometown!

Some women might have found it funny or at least accepted the fashion faux pas gracefully, but Craig's mother just couldn't. She was clearly ill at ease standing next to her peach twin in the receiving line, and left the reception early.

❤ ❤ ❤

WEDDING PORTRAIT
Queen Victoria-Eugenie's Violent Procession

❤ ❤ ❤

On the wedding day of Queen Victoria-Eugenie of Spain, a granddaughter of Queen Victoria, extremists in Madrid threw a bomb at the bridal procession. Before attending her own wedding reception, a shaken but regal queen had to change out of her blood-spattered white satin gown.

No one was hurt when an electrical fire swept through a bridal salon in New York during business hours. But most of the gowns were ruined and had to be promptly replaced by the manufacturers.

One dress was saved, however—by the bride herself. In the salon being fitted for her wedding a week away, she left her clothes to perish in the blaze and ran into the street wearing her gown, sparing it from the flames.

❤ ❤ ❤

Molly wasn't upset that her 11 bridesmaids showed up at her June wedding in casual warm-weather clothing. After all, it *was* summertime in Texas, and the atten-

dants *were* planning on changing before the ceremony—
if their custom-made dresses ever arrived.

"Half of the gowns were delivered to the church just
when the ceremony was scheduled to begin," says Molly,
"but the others never showed up." What did the remaining casually clad bridesmaids do? They threw themselves on the mercy of several well-dressed women guests,
who accommodatingly agreed to exchange clothes.

❤ ❤ ❤

Geraldine, a bride from New York, was convinced she
could diet her way into her wedding dress. The diet was
only partially successful—but she managed to squeeze
into the garment anyway.

During the first dance, however, Geraldine raised her
arms to put them around her new husband, and the nylon
zipper could no longer take the considerable stress and burst.

The bride, now in tears at the back office of the catering hall, begged the banquet manager to do something.
The manager responded with an elegantly engineered
solution—she sewed the back of the poor girl's dress
right to her long-line bra.

❤ ❤ ❤

As Marion stepped out of the limousine at her New
York wedding, her older sister and matron of honor,
Dawn, came to assist her.

With the best intentions, the matron of honor
reached up to adjust the bride's headpiece. As she did
so, however, she stepped on the cathedral train of the

WEDDING PORTRAIT
Queen Victoria's Train Collision

❤ ❤ ❤

When Queen Victoria married Albert of Saxe-Coburg on February 10, 1840, her train measured eighteen feet. That may seem excessively long, but there wasn't enough of it for the twelve bridesmaids to carry down the aisle without causing a pileup. Lady Wilhelmina Stanhope, who was later the Duchess of Cleveland, reported that the bridesmaids "were all huddled together, and scrambled rather than walked along, kicking each other's heels and treading on each other's gowns."

custom-made wedding gown and, with her high heel, ripped a foot-wide hole in the layered netting.

"It won't show," Dawn said hopefully.

But unbeknownst to them both, a stray rose had somehow fallen into the gap in the back of her gown, highlighting the tear. As Marion made her way down the aisle, each row of guests burst into laughter. Midway through the ceremony, the women's mother got up from her seat to remove the offending flower.

Janet and her bridesmaid were putting on the final touches of lipstick in the dressing room of a California church, when the tube slipped from the maid's hands. It bounced down the front of Janet's pure white dress, leaving a trail of waxy crimson from bodice to hem.

There was no time to be hysterical. A dose of club soda and a few puff-fuls of white dusting powder erased most of the telltale stains, and the bride and maid swore each other to secrecy.

And no one found them out—although later on that evening, the mother of the bride did remark to her daughter that she didn't remember the front of the gown being such a *lovely* shade of blush pink.

❤ ❤ ❤

The wedding gown looked beautiful in the bridal shop, but no one had stopped to think that on the day of the wedding, the helpful bridal assistant would not be there to tie the voluminous and absolutely critical bow in back. When the moment of truth arrived at Greta's old-fashioned country wedding in Michigan, everyone was all thumbs. Neither the bride, her mother, nor any of her maids could tie a decent bow.

The bride could not bear the thought of standing at the altar while an entire church gawked at her wilted bow. In desperation, the attendants sent the bride's sister out into the pews to discreetly recruit a guest who could tie a perfect bow. Who finally saved the day? It was none other than the bride's uncle—who tied a beauty and earned a special bridal hug.

❤ ❤ ❤

First, Paula asked her sister, Barbara, to be her matron of honor at her wedding. A month later, Barbara called with good news—she was pregnant! Unfortunately, her delivery date would be too close to the wedding date to guarantee her presence.

The bride next asked a good friend to be her matron of honor. A few weeks later, the friend called back to announce that she was pregnant, too—but not to worry, she would stay in the wedding. Paula was so relieved that she didn't think about how much of a challenge it would be to fit an ever-expanding attendant. The bridal salon had to wait several months to place the dress order while they waited for her size to stabilize.

Meanwhile, more joyous events were being announced left and right: First, another bridesmaid got pregnant. Then, the minister told her that she was expecting, too!

At least the bride showed some restraint. She got pregnant on her honeymoon.

❤ ❤ ❤

Gina had hung her freshly steamed and pressed wedding gown in her closet, but she couldn't resist trying it on one more time before the wedding. To her dismay, she discovered that she was intensely allergic to the cleaning treatment used on the lace neckline. She didn't want to itch and sneeze her way down the aisle, so the lace was removed and the gown completely redesigned two days before the wedding.

Veil of Tears

Five minutes before heading down the aisle, Susanna looked in the mirror. Her flowers were glorious, her dress was suitable for a fairy-tale princess, her makeup was model-perfect, her hair was beautifully coiffed, and on top of her head sat a veil of cascading illusion.

All she had to do was go to the bathroom.

Maneuvering into the stall was no problem. But there was so much material to gather up around her, and when she heard the first strains of the "Wedding March" coming from the church organ, Susanna panicked. She flushed in haste, completely forgetting about all the material on her head.

A struggle ensued between the bride and the inexorable forces of the toilet, with Susanna blindly determined not to let her treasured veil be swept away to some distant sewage-treatment plant. But her tug-of-war only succeeded in clogging the plumbing, and she soon sadly realized that whatever she could salvage probably wouldn't be that fetching anyway.

Susanna's hairstylist improvised a flower headpiece from a few blossoms plucked from the bouquet, and after a brief hiatus, the bride—now much relieved in more ways than one—began her walk down the aisle.

❤ ❤ ❤

A white satin aisle-runner covered the aisle of the New Jersey church. As the bride walked toward the altar with her father, the stiletto heel of her white satin shoe pierced the fabric of the runner and somehow became stuck. The bride paused in what she hoped was a discreet manner and pulled up with her foot. The shoe would not budge. Not wishing to get down on her hands and knees and pull further, she slipped her foot from the shoe and proceeded up the aisle without it.

As knights had been tempted by the Sword Excalibur, so now was the photographer determined to extricate the designer shoe. But, though he tugged and tugged, the shoe resisted him. Sensing that guests had stopped paying attention to the ceremony and begun to watch him, he gave up his quest and left the shoe seemingly cemented in satin in the middle of the aisle.

The aisle now became a kind of obstacle for the recessing bridal party, with the bride, groom, four bridesmaids, and four ushers trying to both ignore the shoe and skirt around it. The bride exited happily on her groom's arm . . . still wearing only one white satin shoe.

❤ ❤ ❤

Jennifer hung her wedding gown and veil in the guest room of a Connecticut inn where she would be married later that August morning. While she and her mother were bustling in and out, taking care of last-minute details, friends of the bride were streaming into her dressing room to look in the bag that held the precious gown and veil.

An hour before the ceremony, the bride was ready to dress. The bride's mother removed the protective bag and her heart sunk. The veil had a large, jagged tear, probably put there when one of the many eager fingers that had reached into the bag had jarred the hanger,

---

WEDDING PORTRAIT
Queen Elizabeth's Snappy Tiara

❤ ❤ ❤

On November 20, 1947, Princess Elizabeth and Philip, Duke of Edinburgh, were married. The princess arrived, calm and composed despite a stressful morning. Moments before her tiara was to be secured to her veil, the band had snapped, necessitating a last-minute call for a jeweler who made palace calls. Then, the princess realized she had misplaced her bouquet. The palace was searched from top to bottom, and the bouquet finally located in a refrigerator, where a concerned footman had placed it to keep it fresh.

causing it to slip and cut a noticeable slice through the tulle.

There was no time for repairs, so the mother of the bride (a wedding consultant by profession) boldly decided a redesign was in order. With needle and thread, the inventive pair quickly gathered poufs in the two sides. Then, they picked out a few white roses from the pails of fresh flowers cooling in the bathroom and attached them to the poufs. No one but Jennifer and her mom were ever the wiser.

❤ ❤ ❤

Frances, a maid of honor in a wedding in North Carolina, borrowed two petticoats for the bridesmaids several days before the big event. But when the wedding day arrived and the women put on the petticoats, they discovered that both of them hung several inches below the hems of their dresses! Luckily, Frances had brought along a spool of white thread and a needle. All it took was a quick basting job to put the petticoats where they belonged—undercover.

❤ ❤ ❤

Adrienne was leaving her home in New York to drive to her church wedding ceremony, when her cat, Maisie, jumped onto her retreating veil as it trailed across the kitchen floor. By the time her mother detached Maisie from the tulle, the cat's claws had rendered the veil utterly unsalvageable.

Adrienne and her parents jumped into the limousine

and made a pit stop at the nearest bridal salon. The startled owners watched as a woman in full bridal dress whirled into the store, shopped for a headpiece, and wore it out the door.

❤ ❤ ❤

WEDDING PORTRAIT
The Nuptials of Katharine Worsley, Future Duchess of Kent

❤ ❤ ❤

When Katharine Worsley married Edward, the Duke of Kent (cousin of Queen Elizabeth II), on June 8, 1961, many thought that the fifteen-foot satin-edged double train on the bride's John Cavanagh gown would cause trouble—it was too long to kneel, stand, and curtsy in. On her wedding day, though, it was actually the bride's expansive tulle veil that got caught on the altar steps of York Minster.

Katharine reacted to the potential catastrophe calmly. She remained in the same position, gazing into her groom's eyes and smiling, until the veil was freed and she could continue through the church.

In California, no one had noticed that there was one nail sticking up through the aisle runner just high enough to snag the bride's cathedral veil. But sure enough, it hooked onto the tulle, pulled it taut, and yanked the headpiece off the bride's formally upswept hair.

Guests gasped as the bride ran back down the aisle and into the dressing room—was she leaving the building in shame? Not at all. The hairstylist recoiffed her hair and repositioned the veil. Simultaneously, a hotel employee hammered in the problem nail. Within fifteen minutes, Stephanie took her place at the rear of the ballroom and restarted her grand march to the altar—this time without incident.

❤ ❤ ❤

On wedding morning, Roberta's brother carefully stowed her makeup, shoes, hose, slip, underwear, and hoop for her elaborate *Gone With the Wind*–style wedding dress in the trunk of his car. Roberta held her gown—lovingly wrapped in plastic—on her lap.

The two arrived at the Alaska church well ahead of schedule. The bride jumped out and ran inside while her brother took off for a prewedding breakfast. Both forgot that all of Roberta's essential bridal accoutrements were still in the trunk.

But Roberta remembered soon enough. Desperate, she called the state highway patrol to try to track her brother down. They refused. Finally, the brother showed up at the church with the much-needed bridal accessories—a scant five minutes before the ceremony was due to begin.

Hoop and all, Roberta walked down the aisle and made it through her vows uneventfully. Such was not the case for her groom, Frank, worn out by the previous evening's bachelor-party festivities, who fainted before he could say "I do." The ceremony was delayed one more time while he revived.

Groomed for Disaster

So conscientious was the groom that he arrived early to inspect the arrangements at the New York synagogue and make sure everything was set up as planned. About a half hour before the service was to begin, he went into a back room to change into his tuxedo—and realized that he had been so busy attending to details that he had forgotten it! The organist noticed that while the ceremony was scheduled to begin any minute, the groom was helplessly pacing the floor in jeans and a sweatshirt. He approached the young man, who explained the situation. The organist immediately offered his own tuxedo. The screen set up around the organ made for a makeshift changing room, and the groom slipped into the borrowed clothing and ran to meet his bride. Still hidden from sight, the generous organist commenced his playing of the "Wedding March"—in his underwear.

♥ ♥ ♥

It was Jeremy's wedding day, and the Wisconsin groom opened his drawer to discover that he had only red-banded gym socks to wear with his tuxedo. Knowing

that his bride would never forgive him, he quickly for-
mulated a plan. Jeremy cut off the red tops of the socks,
and taped the now ragged-edged—but undeniably all
white—socks to his calves.

The improvisatory footwear was going to be Jeremy's
little secret, but the groom was so proud of himself he
just couldn't stay mum. In fact, all day long he kept
raising his pants legs to show off his handiwork to the
guests—and the photographer.

❤ ❤ ❤

The bride was wondering if she'd be left at the altar,
when the groom and the best man came tearing up in the
best man's car. After the groom alighted, the best man
slammed the car door shut behind him—catching the
groom's trousers in the latch and ripping them down the
back.

"Don't give it a second thought!" declared the best
man in the finest best-man tradition. "Take mine!" With
that, both men removed their trousers and traded.

And so, instead of standing up for his buddy, the best
man crouched in the bushes outside the church until the
service began, then went into the church's dressing
rooms in search of some intact britches.

❤ ❤ ❤

An ensign in the navy, Jason had it all planned out.
He had requested shore leave for the morning of the
wedding, and once he left his ship dockside, he would

have six hours to make the five-hour drive to the church in Alabama. Charlotte, his bride, wondered how he would ever make it on time, but Jason reassured her. If a navy man couldn't handle it, who could?

But Jason had forgotten to factor in naval bureaucracy. When the morning arrived, his commanding officers spent two hours sorting out the shore-leave list. The groom was finally dismissed with just four hours to get to the church on time. Jason sped all the way, arriving only twenty minutes late.

Since Jason was already in his uniform, he raced up the church steps—only to stop dead in his tracks. He hadn't tied his tie. It was such a simple thing—well within the capabilities of a navy man—but by this point the nervous and exhausted Jason was all thumbs. Try as he might, his tie would not tie.

Ten minutes went by. Then an observant usher spied the fumbling, frantic groom through the door and came out to assist him. Strains of the "Wedding March" wafted out onto the street just thirty minutes behind schedule.

❤ ❤ ❤

Relations between Charlene's divorced parents were not cordial. Her father was not involved in any of the plans, and decided not to attend his daughter's Michigan wedding. Faced with walking alone down the aisle, the bride enlisted her Uncle Fred to be her escort.

Uncle Fred was honored—and so conscientious! He paid careful attention to the minister's instructions at the run-through, and even toasted the bride at the rehearsal dinner. The next day, the wedding consultant finished lining up the attendants and looked around for Uncle Fred. Five minutes before the ceremony was to begin, she spotted him getting out of his car—wearing a plaid polyester suit!

The wedding was formal. The bridesmaids were dressed in lavender floor-length gowns, the groomsmen in tuxedos. "You can't escort the bride wearing a plaid suit!" the wedding consultant told him.

"I know," said Uncle Fred, grinning. "There's been a change in plans. The bride's father will escort her." Oh my God, thought the consultant. If this is the uncle, what could the father be wearing?

At that minute, the surprise escort appeared on the church steps—dressed in a proper tuxedo and bow tie.

❤ ❤ ❤

Beth and John arrived at the church in Maine fifteen minutes before their noon ceremony. The guests were arriving too—in a steady stream. Where were the ushers?

The bridesmaids told them. Late that morning, the groomsmen realized that it was their responsibility, not the groom's, to rent formal shirts. The group piled into a car and burned rubber to the nearest shopping mall. But the mall was forty-five minutes away in good traffic conditions—and traffic conditions were not good that day.

Noon came, and with no ushers in sight, the guests had seated themselves. By two o'clock, the bride's mother was insisting that the ceremony get underway, ushers or no ushers.

The procession began, when the sound of screeching tires rang out. The men had arrived! Jumping out of the car, their hair still wet from showers, they rushed into position and marched down the aisle—out of breath, but undeniably dapper.

❤ ❤ ❤

Jeff never realized that his army buddies had made off with his shoes the night before the wedding. But when Jeff knelt at the altar in Texas with his bride, Susie, guests seated in the front pews knew something had been afoot: on the left sole was scrawled HELP and on the right, ME.

❤ ❤ ❤

During an Indiana ceremony in 1984, the maid of honor was startled to notice that through the groom's white pants she could see colored stripes circling his mid-calf. During the picture-taking session, she leaned over and asked the groom about his footwear; he explained that he couldn't find a pair of white socks to match his tuxedo that morning, so he made do with a pair that had yellow-and-blue stripes. When he lifted his pants legs to show her, the entire wedding party broke into laughter, and the photographer captured it on film.

❤ ❤ ❤

Naturally, Bill didn't want his tuxedo to get wrinkled or soiled before the ceremony began, so he put his entire

WEDDING PORTRAIT
Count Leo Tolstoy Weds Sofya Andreevna Bers

❤ ❤ ❤

The Russian Orthodox Church of the Virgin Birth in the Kremlin was the setting for Count Leo Tolstoy's marriage to Sofya Bers on September 23, 1862. The liturgy required the groom to arrive at the church first, then send the best man to signal the bride to journey to the church to join him. Though Sofya was a nervous bride, she was dressed, veiled, and waiting. After an hour and a half, she could only think the worst.

But she hadn't been left at the altar. The man who was to write *War and Peace* and *Anna Karenina* had packed his formal shirt in a trunk stored at the bride's home. Finally, a servant arrived to retrieve the shirt. The reassured bride was soon summoned to the ceremony.

ensemble in the car and donned jeans and a sweatshirt for the long drive to the country inn where he would marry Sylvia.

But once he had changed into his formal wear in the

room set aside for him, he realized he had forgotten one crucial accessory: the shoes. In vain, he phoned his home and friends—everyone was already on the way to the ceremony.

So the groom wore tennis shoes down the aisle. And even the bride was a good sport about it.

♥ ♥ ♥

Twenty minutes before his wedding in Alabama was to begin, Stu zipped up his tux pants, only to have the fly break. There was no time to have a new zipper put in, and safety pins left gaps.

Stu's grandmother got her sewing kit and took drastic action: she stitched the fly of the pants closed. Stu kept his grandmother's handiwork intact throughout the reception—and kept his intake of champagne to a minimum.

♥ ♥ ♥

The bride and groom packed their bags and stowed them in the groom's car the morning of their mansion wedding in New York City. They planned to depart for their honeymoon immediately after the ceremony.

That afternoon, the car was stolen. The groom spent hours trying to track the vehicle down, so he only had a short time to rush back to his apartment to pick up his tuxedo and get to the ceremony. Then he realized his apartment key was in the stolen car.

At a loss, in more ways than one, he nevertheless went to the mansion in his sweats, having no idea where he would get formal attire. A kindhearted waiter came to the rescue: he loaned the hapless groom his own tuxedo—even though it meant being consigned to the kitchen for the rest of the evening.

❤ WEDDING FROM HELL NO. 2 ❤

The morning of Jason's wedding, he received a call from his bride, Penny. She had just had a horrific fight with her sister, whose husband, Jim, had come to his wife's defense by pushing Penny and knocking her down. Jason rushed over to Penny's house and found her sitting on the front steps in her wedding gown, sobbing. The bride's brother-in-law had to be forcefully separated from a fistfight with Jim.

The groom loaded the bride and her luggage into his car and drove her to his house. While he went to change into his formal wear at his sister's house, his mother called to reroute the flower delivery and photographer to the new address.

When the wedding party arrived at the church, it was obvious that the priest was intoxicated. He left out all of the hymns selected by the couple and never asked them to read the vows they had written for the ceremony. Finally, the disoriented officiant pronounced them husband and wife.

They exited the church on that 100-degree summer afternoon only to discover that their limousine had overheated. Repeated efforts to start the engine proved futile, so the limousine driver gathered up Penny's train in one hand and stopped traffic with the other. The trio crossed the busy thoroughfare and walked to the reception hall.

They arrived, hot and flustered, only to be told that the air-conditioning in the building had shorted out. Jason's uncle, a wedding guest, came to the rescue. Owner of a refrigeration business, he took off his suit coat and went to work on the system.

Cool air began circulating again, and all the anger that had accumulated during the day cooled down considerably—except between the bride and her sister, who still barely talk to one another.

CHAPTER 3

The Best-Laid Plans . . .

A wedding ceremony is a fairy-tale moment
of romance and candlelight built on a foundation of lists and schedules for every mun-
dane eventuality.

—From *BRIDE'S* magazine

❤ ❤ ❤

The Wrong Place at the Wrong Time

Everything about the wedding cake was wonderful. Outside was delectable chocolate icing, the groom's favorite. Inside the sweet sensation was banana cake, the bride's favorite. All three tiers were covered with delicate spun-sugar flowers in lavender, echoing the color of the bridesmaids' gowns. And on the top, elegantly written in ivory and taupe icing, were the names Malcolm and Rose.

The bride and groom's names were Amanda and Charles.

The mistake was caught by the bridal consultant a half hour before the Connecticut reception was to start. The chef could smooth over Malcolm and Rose, but he didn't have any icing to write the actual bride's and groom's names.

Did Amanda and Charles complain about having a cake with no names? How could they? By the time they arrived at the reception, the chef had found another writing implement—traditional wedding almonds.

❤ ❤ ❤

The ushers were anxiously waiting for the mother of the groom to arrive at the church in Connecticut. The ceremony was about to begin and they still had to escort her to her seat of honor.

The door opened and the formally dressed wedding consultant appeared, planning to take a final head count of the guests. Despite her whispered protests, a persistent usher hustled her down the center aisle to a front pew.

After waiting a few interminable minutes, the consultant rose with great dignity, walked down a side aisle, and made a fast getaway out of the sanctuary. The real mother of the groom arrived shortly thereafter, and to the guests' amusement, she was speedily seated in the same location by the same overly zealous usher.

❤ ❤ ❤

Nearly two hundred wedding guests awaited the first glimpse of the bride at the rear of the ballroom in an elegant California hotel. The doors swung open, and a loud gasp traveled through every pew. She was beautiful, to be sure—but no one recognized her.

She was at the wrong wedding.

Poor Mara was just as confused as the guests. Not only was there no huppah for the Jewish ceremony she was expecting—but the groom she saw waiting for her at the end of the aisle was a total stranger!

After what seemed like hours, a hotel staff member appeared and led the bride to *her* ceremony and guests—waiting in another part of the building.

❤ ❤ ❤

The band had been playing at the wedding for an hour and a half when the bride's father approached the bandstand.

"Thank you so much for playing for us," he said, "but why are you here?"

The bride's father had thought the band was a gift from the groom's family. But he was wrong—and so was the band. They had been booked to play at the country-club lodge, and had gone to the clubhouse instead.

The band quickly broke down their equipment and made a beeline for the right site—an hour late, perhaps, but better late than never.

❤ ❤ ❤

Connie decided to follow family tradition and wear her mother's wedding gown to her own ceremony in Texas. Last worn by a cousin four years earlier, the silk-taffeta and tulle dress with lace appliqués now hung in a spare-bedroom closet, nestled in an opaque bag that had not been opened since it had returned from the cleaner's.

Mother and daughter now lovingly opened the bag—and discovered that they had been given the wrong dress!

The cleaner was appalled as well, and immediately went back into his files, calling all the clients who had brought in wedding gowns four years ago.

The right dress was eventually located, and the

cleaner arranged to make the switch. But the other customer was not nearly as anxious to have her long-lost wedding gown back. *Her* daughter, who had worn the dress, was already divorced.

❤ ❤ ❤

The bride and groom didn't want a moment without music at their wedding. The ceremony and the reception were to be held in a hotel suite in California, and three groups of musicians were booked for the event. A string quartet was to play before and during the ceremony, and two bands—one Caribbean, one swing—were to play at the reception.

When the bands arrived at the suite, they thought things seemed a little quiet, but went ahead and set up their equipment anyway. The time for the wedding drew near, but no one else arrived.

The musicians got nervous. Just then, a passing busboy stuck his head in the room and asked, "You here for the Hopkins wedding?"

The bandleader nodded, the busboy laughed and then said, "Well, they moved the ceremony to the cathedral up the street!"

The string quartet jumped up, grabbed their instruments, and piled into the bandleader's van. Violin bows and spare arms were akimbo out the windows, but they made it to the church on time—just minutes before the bride and groom.

❤ ❤ ❤

Penny and Wade sent invitations to 150 guests for their wedding at "The Congregational Church." They didn't realize that there were two congregational churches in the small Connecticut town. As a result, their wedding day was somewhat like stepping into a parallel universe.

Right before the start of her ceremony, Penny's family noticed that at least twenty out-of-town acquaintances hadn't arrived. They had been misdirected to the other church, where they watched a veiled bride come down the aisle and listened to the minister welcome them to the wedding of . . . the wrong couple!

To the consternation of that congregation, twenty guests gasped in unison, got up, and rushed down the center aisle and out of the church. The group marched into Penny and Wade's wedding during the first Scripture reading.

❤ ❤ ❤

When Sharon and Peter were ready to leave their reception at an Oregon restaurant, they gave their car keys to their best man so he could deliver their getaway car to the front door. Then they waited. And waited. And waited some more.

The best man finally returned, looking puzzled. Why didn't the key fit the ignition of the now lavishly festooned bridal car? Then it dawned on another member of the bridal party: they had decorated the wrong vehicle.

It was a natural mistake—most of the guests were from

out of town, everyone was driving rental cars—but that wasn't very much consolation as, in bitingly cold weather, the wedding party tried to undecorate the poor stranger's car, trailing balloons and streamers through the parking lot to the proper automobile. Despite their valiant efforts, there was no doubt that the stranger's car would certainly benefit from a pass through the car wash.

What's the Date?

Josephine was experiencing labor pains and went to the hospital. After examining her, a nurse told the expectant mother that she was in false labor—there would be no arrival that day.

By the ninth month, most women cannot wait to give birth, but Josephine was overjoyed at the delay. She immediately asked the nurse if she could possibly be discharged by the next morning—it was her wedding day!

❤ ❤ ❤

The wedding was scheduled more than a year in advance at an elegant hotel in New York. More than three hundred guests had been invited, and a twenty-piece orchestra was booked to play. Three months before the wedding day, the bride-to-be telephoned the music coordinator to tell her the date had to be moved up. Her original wedding day was now her due date as well!

As the bride grew larger, she deemed it appropriate that the wedding grow smaller. The once-lavish event became an at-home affair with just one hundred guests—and a string quartet instead of an orchestra.

❤ ❤ ❤

When Andrew, 35, a lawyer in Washington, proposed to Barbara in January, they planned an autumn wedding and honeymoon. Soon afterward, the trial date of a very important case that Andrew was due to argue was rescheduled to the day before his honeymoon was to end!

Faced with the possibility of delaying the wedding (not to mention the honeymoon), Andrew put his faith in the American legal system. He filed a formal motion with the trial judge in Federal District Court, pleading that the trial date be further postponed. The following are excerpts from his appeal:

It has taken Counsel over thirty-four years to find someone whom he loves and who loves him.

Scheduling for a wedding, especially one involving the concurrence of two out-of-town families and the Roman Catholic Church, requires considerable advance planning.

On very solid information and belief, Counsel believes that his betrothed will feel very irritated, ignored, and offended if the honeymoon must be canceled, delayed or cut short. Counsel further believes such feelings would be justified.

Counsel is loath to begin what he very sincerely hopes and intends to be his one and only marriage by offending his bride-to-be, in-laws, associated friends, and the Roman Catholic Church.

Accordingly, Counsel respectfully offers the eternal gratitude of himself, his heirs, his assigns, and his issue (if any there be), in return for the Court's compassion.

The judge's response? Well, justice may be blind, but not when it comes to love. An excerpt:

In this Court's twenty years of judicial experience, Counsel's motion for reconsideration is unprecedented in its creativity and its urgency. In a spirit of cooperation with . . . efforts to avoid eternal damnation and to please (and appease) his intended, their families and friends, as well as the Roman Catholic Church, it is hereby ORDERED that the . . . Motion for Reconsideration of Trial Date is GRANTED.

Vows in Unexpected Places

On the night he planned to ask Maria to marry him, Jerry instead went out with the boys and ended up being arrested on a drunk driving charge. Because he had three previous convictions, Jerry was held in a minimum-security prison in lieu of $50,000 bail. He faced sixteen months in prison if convicted on the new charge, but Maria did not want to wait another day to marry him. "Let me tell you," she said, "the guy has charm!"

Their wedding ceremony was held in a visitors' room at the men's barracks. The bride wore a floral dress; the groom sported green prison garb. Why was it so important that they marry on this particular day? It was the fourth anniversary of the day the couple met—and, coincidentally, also Pearl Harbor Day. Asked if the historic event had any bearing in his own day, Jerry dryly replied, "I guess I won't be getting bombed."

❤ ❤ ❤

It was going to be the second marriage for both Judy and Paul. Since Judy's sister was to be married and Judy did not want to steal her thunder, she offered to post-

WEDDING PORTRAIT
Lou Gehrig Shuts Out His Mother

♥ ♥ ♥

From the moment they became engaged, Eleanor and Lou Gehrig, the famous New York Yankee baseball player, knew that Lou's mother would be hard to handle. Prone to tantrums and hysterics, Mrs. Gehrig had a particularly extreme emotional outbreak the day before Eleanor and Lou's scheduled nuptials. Lou rushed to New Rochelle, where Eleanor was moving into their new apartment. Carpet layers, plumbers, telephone installers, and other workers were scurrying about; newly delivered furniture was stacked in corners.

Lou reported that his mother was in an alarming state and would probably not calm down for the wedding day. Rather than risk a scene the next day, they decided to marry then and there. Lou phoned the mayor of New Rochelle, who arrived a short time later with a police escort. With Eleanor in her apron, Lou in his shirtsleeves, and the workers as guests, the mayor performed the marriage. An ersatz reception followed, with champagne (on hand for the next day) quickly chilled with ice rounded up by the janitor.

pone her own wedding for a year. Finally the date was approaching fast—nothing else could stand in their way.

Then, just weeks before the wedding date, Paul was painting the trim on Judy's house. The aluminum ladder he was standing on broke and he fell backward onto the asphalt, landing on his spine. A neighbor eventually heard his cries for help and called an ambulance. Paul had suffered a compound fracture of the spine that required him to stay in bed and wear a cast.

Since he and Judy had already postponed their wedding once, they decided to forge ahead—in the hospital. The couple borrowed a room that was normally used for hospital functions for their reception. Friends and relatives brought potluck meals, and neighbors who hadn't even been invited to the ceremony insisted on setting up and cleaning up.

As for Paul, such was his determination to wed Judy that he managed to get out of his hospital gown and into a real suit and shoes for his big day!

Upstaged

Alice and Chris had scheduled their Texas wedding far in advance—how could they know the December date would coincide with a critical Houston Oilers–Pittsburgh Steelers game?

Avid football fans, the wedding party arrived at the church with radios in tow. But as the ceremony grew closer, so did the score. When it came time to walk down the aisle, the men refused to part with their transistors. The groom, ushers, best man, both fathers, and three grandfathers walked down the aisle with radios tucked inside their tuxedo jackets and wires plugged inside their ears.

When it was time to exchange vows, the minister discreetly turned to Chris and said, "Please take that thing out of your ear." Then, just before he pronounced the couple married, he paused. "I'd like to take a moment to ask you something," he said, looking solemnly at those assembled. "What's the score?"

❤ ❤ ❤

Joan was horrified to see that her younger sister was inserting herself into the middle of virtually every photograph taken at her wedding. "She does this at every family event," she fumed to Richard, her groom.

In desperation, the couple enlisted the aid of the best man. While he kept her occupied for a set of sixties dance tunes, they instructed their photographer to speedily snap the list of group photos they had given him—without the spotlight-stealing sis.

❤ ❤ ❤

While Cameron, a photographer, and Mary Beth, a secretary, certainly considered their wedding important, they hadn't counted on it turning into a major-league event. But during the reception, the bride's father stood up and announced that an autograph table would be set up after the dinner for guests to meet the bride's brother, a major-league baseball player. Neither the bride nor her new husband seemed to be irritated by the announcement, nor by the fact the festivities were held up a good half hour while children and adults lined up for autographs.

❤ ❤ ❤

The bride, groom, and their families had gathered in the hallway of a large catering hall in New York to pose for a group portrait. Just as the photographer began shooting, he saw the expressions on the faces of his subjects turn to fear and disgust. Turning around, he saw that a rat the size of a pussycat had wandered from behind a curtain toward the group and was now regarding them calmly. Hearing the commotion, the caterer came out, sized up the situation, and left for the kitchen. He returned with the top of a chafing dish, deftly placed it over the animal, and, without a word, went back to work.

Missing Persons

The morning of their wedding in California, Tara and Joe arrived together at the reception hall, already dressed in gown and tuxedo. Their wedding party was also there, and together they primped and awaited the arrival of their 150 guests.

There was one little mishap: the maid of honor's hem came undone. Tara sent her groom-to-be out to the store for some straight pins. He jumped into his car and sped away.

An extreme attack of cold feet must have occurred somewhere between the store and the church, because Joe never came back. Not only was the maid's hem left hanging—so was the bride!

❤ ❤ ❤

It was autumn. The wedding procession in the Texas hotel ballroom was about to begin. The bridal party stood poised in the foyer. The singer was well into "And This Is My Beloved." Then the clergyman noticed that one of the beloved was missing—the groom.

He passed a note to the soloist. KEEP SINGING, it read.

CAN'T FIND THE GROOM. Then he sent an usher up to the groomsmen's suite on the twenty-fourth floor. There, a nonchalant groom was found watching football. His excuse? "I was waiting for someone to come get me."

Steve was hustled out of the room and escorted downstairs, where he took his position on the line of bridal scrimmage.

❤ ❤ ❤

An hour and a half after the "Wedding March" should have started, Anita began to realize that Carlos, her groom, would not be coming to their church wedding in New York. Although she was devastated, nothing could compare to the way her grandmother, and the groom's grandmother, took the news. Loud Spanish epithets were shouted from one side of the aisle to the other. The bride's granny ordered Anita's brother to quickly carry the wedding gifts out to their car—before the *other* granny could get her hands on them!

❤ ❤ ❤

The bride was an Italian Catholic, the groom a Mediterranean Jew. The groom's family and community had forbidden him to marry outside his faith, but he was determined to wed the woman he loved.

On the day of the wedding, the limousine hired by the catering hall in California proceeded to the motel where the groom was supposed to be waiting—or, rather, *hiding* from his family until the ceremony. But when the limo driver walked up to the door, he saw that it had been kicked in. Inside the room, the telephone had been ripped out of the wall, and there were signs of a struggle.

The driver suspected foul play; it was a shrewd deduction. The groom's parents had literally had their son kidnapped from the motel. He'd been thrown into the trunk of a car and driven out of state, and the wedding never took place.

❤ ❤ ❤

After the first course of the New York wedding-reception meal, Ida's father was nowhere to be found. The hall threatened to stop serving the rest of the food unless payment in full was received. The bride's father seemed to have left the building, so she and her groom pooled the checks and cash they had received as gifts and handed them over to the caterer.

Two months later, the bride's mother received a letter from the bride's father—postmarked Florida. The explanation? Knowing he didn't have money to pay for the reception, he had fled south in shame.

❤ ❤ ❤

Gwen had already paid her caterers more than five thousand dollars toward the Connecticut reception when, two months before the wedding day, her intended announced that he could not go through with it. The caterer was willing to refund only a small portion of the fee, which meant that the agreed-upon menu—hors d'oeuvres, fruit cup, garden salad, chicken, string beans, baked potato, and cake and ice cream—was going to be paid for, no matter what.

Not wanting the food to go to waste, the bride decided to go ahead with the reception, sans wedding ceremony, and invite the truly needy. Contacting the local shelters in her Connecticut town, Gwen informed them that she had places for 150 guests, and asked only that they make reservations.

"This is better than a wedding," the bride gamely declared, as she watched her guests enjoying the meal, and accepted several of their invitations to dance.

Bridal Pinch Hitters

The bride was much impressed with the innovative young caterer referred to her by the staff at the Victorian mansion where her wedding would be held. For months they worked side-by-side, planning a mouth-watering menu that would perfectly capture the turn-of-the-century ambience she wanted.

As the wedding drew nearer, she realized that the one thing she wanted was not on the menu. Her family and friends were shocked when she canceled the wedding just days ahead of time . . . and ran off with the caterer.

❤ ❤ ❤

Liza and her wedding guests were eagerly awaiting the arrival of her Indian prince, who was flying in from London for their wedding ceremony at an exclusive country club in California.

The time for the groom's arrival had long passed, and the bride realized she had been stood up. It would have been utterly humiliating—but it dawned on Liza that none of her guests had ever met the errant prince. The wedding—or at least the appearance of one—could go on after all. Borrowing a ring from the wedding consultant, she married her elegantly uniformed limo driver. The wedding was invalid, of course, but no one found out her cleverly staged charade that day.

❤ ❤ ❤

Yvonne and Tony scheduled their June wedding at a catering hall in the neighboring New York town well in advance. About six months before the day, they met with the banquet manager and carefully plotted the details of their reception.

Two months later, they called back. The wedding would have to be postponed until August—but all the arrangements would remain the same. In May, Yvonne telephoned the banquet manager and told him that the wedding was again being postponed—this time until October. They would make a few changes in colors to better suit the seasons. Other than that, all arrangements would remain the same.

In September, the banquet manager received another phone call, this time from the groom-to-be. "I'm marrying a different girl," Tony told him. "Other than that, all the arrangements will remain the same!"

Logistical Snafus

Joshua had given Matthew, his best man, all the keys to the caravan of wedding cars. The wedding party and out-of-town guests were now waiting to be driven to the country-club reception. But where was Matthew?

After fifteen minutes, the groom ran up the steps of the church and found his best man sitting in a rear pew—talking with a long-lost girlfriend. Matthew had spotted her among the guests coming through the receiving line in the church vestibule. He discovered that she had gone to school with the bride. Eager to rekindle the romance, he had lost all sense of time, place, and responsibility.

The keys, the best man, and true love finally found, the motors were revved and the caravan went on its way.

❤ ❤ ❤

Maybe having eight hundred guests wasn't such a great idea after all. At Claudia and Ryan's Texas reception, the receiving line took so long that guests began to help themselves to the buffet, find their places at their tables, and eat dinner. The line was still in full force by the time many of them had finished.

Those who had dined waited, hoping to see the bride and groom have their first dance and cut the cake. But as time passed and the receiving line showed no signs of drawing to an end, many guests left without having any dessert.

❤ ❤ ❤

To give members of the wedding party a moment in the spotlight, Laurie and Steve requested that the disc jockey at their New York wedding introduce everyone individually. Bob, the DJ, was happy to comply. He took Laurie and Steve's list of the bridesmaids' and ushers' names and gave it to the banquet manager, whose job was to line up the couples in order outside in the hallway before their grand entrance.

Since the whole thing was being videotaped, Bob wanted to make a big show of each announcement. But it quickly became apparent that although the banquet manager may have known catering, people were not his strong suit: all the men were misaligned.

And so, when maid-of-honor Cheryl and best-man Bill walked in, Bob consulted his list for the correct names and announced with a flourish, "And he-ere's Cheryl and *Jim*."

Next came Julie and Bryan, introduced by Bob as Julie and *Evan*. And so on down the line, each bridesmaid was introduced by her right name, each groomsman by someone else's.

❤ ❤ ❤

Brittany, a bride from Michigan, arrived at her reception site the morning before her ceremony to find it filled with construction equipment. Once she was told that the equipment was there for better or worse, she decided to work with the unexpected props as best she could.

The bride dashed to her printer to order signs that said, SORRY, WE DIDN'T PLAN THIS. The day of the wedding, she attached small bouquets of flowers to the signs and positioned them on the construction equipment. Guests were so impressed, they made lots of "constructive" comments throughout the hors d'oeuvres.

❤ ❤ ❤

The perfect seating plan for two hundred wedding guests: Rebecca and Evan spent a month drawing up and analyzing lists, trying to achieve it. Finally, they had twenty-five tables of eight—a perfect grouping of ages, occupations, and interests.

At the reception, when Rebecca's Uncle Joe came through the receiving line, he had already picked up his table card. "Why aren't my two sons seated at my table?" he asked angrily. Patiently, the bride explained that Evan's fraternity brothers were the same age, and that her cousins would have a great time at their table. She apologized, but firmly told her uncle that it was too late to change the seating plan.

But Uncle Joe was determined to have his way. He strode into the ballroom of the hotel, picked up two place settings from a nearby table, squeezed them onto his table, and moved the chairs over as well. Then he had his two sons sit down with him.

The final two guests who arrived at the table saw that it was full. Thinking that a mistake had been made, they simply moved over to another table where there were extra seats. Soon the seating problem turned into a chain reaction throughout the room. Every table was short two seats, and guests moved to other tables at random.

Who ended up with the boisterous frat boys? None other than the groom's boss and his wife.

The bride was in tears, but Uncle Joe had a great time. After all, he had his family gathered about him.

❤ ❤ ❤

A sumptuous estate in California was the perfect evening wedding site for Jennifer and Lawrence. Guests would feast on hors d'oeuvres in the mansion's wood-paneled library, then proceed to an outdoor tent for a formal seated dinner.

When members of the bridal party arrived in advance for prereception photographs, however, they found an empty patio covered in scaffolding. Ladders were strewn everywhere. There was no tent, no dance floor, no tables, no chairs, and no lighting.

Knowing that the newlyweds would be disappointed

and angry, everyone pitched in to erect the tent before the bride, groom, and first guests filed in. The ushers made a quick trip to the local school next door to borrow seating. The maid of honor made a frantic call to the florist to request hundreds of candles to illuminate the tent. And the bridesmaids did some deft tucking and folding of the too-big linens that were available.

Guests and newlyweds never even thought to ask about the delay. Those in the know just kept them plied with champagne in the library until things were in place outside.

❤ ❤ ❤

Gayle was the director of a senior citizen's program in New York. It seemed natural to her and Jay that she invite the members of the group to the prewedding cocktail hour and to the ceremony at the synagogue. To make travel as easy as possible, she rented a school bus to pick up the fifty seniors at their homes and drop them off early in the evening, before the reception.

The elderly ladies and gentlemen had a wonderful time, thanked Gayle, and then reboarded the bus for home. The dinner dance was well underway when Gayle noticed that the bus driver had returned. One of the elderly passengers was still on board—a woman who couldn't remember her address. With nowhere to leave her, the driver had brought her back to the reception.

The bride draped her long train across her arm and boarded the bus with her groom. Dora, who had been too frightened to leave her seat before, relaxed as soon

WEDDING PORTRAIT
The Nuptials of Jessie Woodrow Wilson

♥ ♥ ♥

November 25, 1913, was the wedding day of Jessie Woodrow Wilson, President Woodrow Wilson's middle daughter, to law student Francis Bowes Sayre. The couple followed the tradition of not seeing each other until the ceremony.

Frank and his best man had taken a walk and returned in time to dress and drive to the White House. When they arrived, the front-gate guard could not be convinced that Frank was the groom; neither Frank nor his best man had an invitation or any other proof with them. Frank pleaded that the wedding couldn't take place without him. "You'll have to tell that to the captain," said the guard. "I have my orders, and this is a very special White House occasion."

Finally, when the captain was summoned at Frank's request, he listened to the story and allowed the groom to attend his own wedding.

as she saw a familiar face. She agreed to get off the bus, and she told Gayle where she had to go. Alternate transportation for the confused guest was found—the souped-up car of a teenager employed by the caterer. Convincing her it was safe to get in took another fifteen minutes. All told, they missed an hour of their wedding—but Dora got home safe and sound.

❤ ❤ ❤

Melanie, a maid of honor at her best friend's wedding in North Carolina, realized as she was walking down the aisle that she had neglected to remind the ushers to light the two altar candles. As the wedding party filed before the officiant at the altar, she caught the best man's eye, and then pointed to the unlit candles. During the minister's prayer, the best man calmly walked out to the guests in the pews, borrowed a lighter, lit the candles, and stepped back into place. The bride and groom lit their unity candle as planned and never noticed the fast save.

❤ ❤ ❤

Everyone was silent with awe as the bride walked down the aisle of her country-club wedding in New Jersey. The respectful silence continued as the minister began to speak. But the minister was silent, too—the banquet manager had neglected to pin a microphone on him.

The music coordinator ran to remedy the situation with another microphone, at which point the entire sound system broke. The minister, a soft-spoken man

WEDDING PORTRAIT
Rita Hayworth Weds Aly Khan of Yakimour

♥ ♥ ♥

The press had harassed Rita Hayworth throughout her romance with Aly Khan of Yakimour, especially faulting the actress for gallivanting with her lover around the world with her four-year-old daughter in tow. The couple wanted a private ceremony at Aly Khan's Chateau de L'Horizon, away from prying eyes.

French law required weddings take place in public, but Khan thought he could persuade French authorities to allow a private wedding and so printed up invitations for May 27, 1949, at the Chateau. A reporter's protest influenced the judge, however, and their ceremony site shifted to Town Hall in the tiny town of Vallauris.

As required by law, royalty and peasants alike were allowed to witness the rite. Reporters, who were barred at first, were also allowed in—if they behaved.

Someone didn't behave, however. Hayworth's white Cadillac convertible had to be repainted before it could be used for the wedding. En route from the United States, it had been covered with graffiti—greetings to the sultry actress from her fans.

who mumbled, continued the service, even though none of the guests could hear a thing. As a result, three hundred frustrated guests began buzzing and talking, and no one had the slightest idea of what stage the ceremony was at until the groom kissed the bride.

❤ ❤ ❤

It was one of those torrid California days, and the reception was set for outdoors. Everything seemed in place except for one crucial ingredient: the champagne. Against the consultant's better judgment, the bride's father had put himself in charge of supplying the bubbly.

The time arrived for the toasting to begin, and the father of the bride—and his 150 bottles of champagne—were nowhere to be found. Well, thought the consultant desperately, he *is* the father of the bride and it *was* a long receiving line and there *were* a lot of pictures to get taken. . . .

So she waited. And the guests waited. And waited. Finally, the consultant couldn't stand it anymore—the weather was sweltering and the festivities would be ruined without champagne. So she sent her assistants out to the local liquor stores to buy up all the bottles of chilled champagne they could find.

Two hours later, Dad arrived. He had gotten into a fender bender on the way from the church. He was unhurt, he said, but very thirsty. Was there any champagne?

Chaos on a Grand Scale

Terry and Joan thought it was an inspired idea: have real doves on hand to bill and coo throughout the ceremony, then release them right after the "I do's," to fly about the New York Hotel ballroom, creating a living, feathered tribute to the couple's love.

And it was just like something out of a romance novel—at first. The wedding guests who had gathered in the ballroom of one of Chicago's big hotels found the gentle cooing ever so sweet, and everyone oohed and aahed as the freed doves soared to the ceiling while Terry and Joan kissed.

But while the doves were more than willing to go up where they belonged (to borrow from a popular wedding song), they were less enthused about coming down. Eluding all attempts to recapture them, they roosted in the chandeliers like a bunch of lovebirds for the duration of the evening—peppering the guests with droppings throughout the seated dinner.

Wendy and Steve planned to release two white doves from a bird cage during the final moments of the New York party—a symbol of how they planned to live in peace and harmony. Unfortunately, one of the waiters had placed the bird cage on a hot grill that had been used to cook crepes for the Viennese dessert table. When the bride and groom opened the cage, the two doves limply flapped out, remained airborne for a moment, and then fell to the floor—roasted.

❤ ❤ ❤

Brenda and Stuart were traveling from their ceremony to their reception in California. A beautiful wedding carriage had been reserved for their journey: the horse had a braided mane and tail and was splendidly attired in a white feathered headpiece.

Video cameras followed every move. But as the carriage pulled away from the church, the horse stopped suddenly, lifted his tail, and defecated for a seemingly interminable length of time. The bride screamed; the groom's face went blank. The horse then pranced on as if nothing had happened, and safely delivered the newly married couple to their reception.

❤ ❤ ❤

Miranda's father meant well, but when his daughter realized that he had hired a comic to perform during their wedding dinner in New York, she blew up in front of all the guests. Just as she began to scream uncontrollably at her father, the lights dimmed and a spotlight focused on the comic. The bride stormed up to the performer and loudly whispered, "Get the f—— off the stage before I kick you in the balls!"

The comic was quick on his feet. "Excuse me, ladies and gentlemen," he said, "but this is no time to linger!"

❤ ❤ ❤

Carol and Daniel of Virginia don't have to work very hard at remembering their wedding. Whenever they hear the national anthem and the line, "the rockets' red glare," they're immediately transported back to a truly unforgettable evening.

In honor of her daughter's marriage, Carol's mother planned to set off fireworks on the lawn of her waterside home. But after the first rocket went off to great applause, the situation became explosive—literally. Something went drastically amiss in the canister holding the remaining ten fireworks, and the rockets suddenly went on a rampage, exploding and shooting off their brilliant lights at random.

One singed Carol's new mother-in-law's hair. Another shot through the tent, and yet another went through the dining room window, setting on fire not only the new carpet, but also a friend's heirloom tablecloth and the wedding gifts sitting on top of it. So deafening was the noise that jets from the nearby naval air station flying overhead broke formation and made a beeline for the base, apparently convinced they were under attack.

Afterward, friends sent the bride's mother specially

made T-shirts that read, "I survived Carol and Daniel's wedding."

❤ ❤ ❤

Becky's mother insisted that the New York florist install fountains on various balconies around the ballroom of the hotel—the sound of trickling water would be lovely during the quiet ceremony, she reasoned.

It also proved an elegant demonstration of the power of suggestion. The photographer noted an unusually large number of the 400 guests slipping out of the ceremony and running to the bathroom.

❤ ❤ ❤

Cecilia had envisioned an elegant garden theme for her reception. She had even rented the Garden Room in one of the California town's deluxe hotels, and proceeded to spare no expense to achieve her idea of perfection: garlands of flowers lacing the chandeliers, white roses in sterling-silver urns on the lace tablecloths.

As for seating, the hotel suggested using elegant upholstered chairs, but Cecilia and her mother were aghast at the idea. Whoever heard of upholstery in a *garden*? Only wicker and bamboo would do. Fortunately, the florist had grasped the concept, and volunteered that he knew just the chair to order.

When Cecilia's mother arrived on the morning of the wedding to inspect the Garden Room, however, she discovered that although the chairs were indeed bamboo-

WEDDING PORTRAIT
The Nuptials of Caroline Kennedy

❤ ❤ ❤

On July 19, 1986, Caroline Kennedy, 28, married Edwin Schlossberg, 42, president of a company that designs museum interiors and exhibits, at Our Lady of Victory Church in Hyannis Port, Massachusetts. As the groom's mother, Mae Schlossberg, left the church, she tripped on the steps, in clear view of many of the four hundred guests. Fortunately, she was more flustered than injured.

The music and dancing went on into the night at the Kennedy compound in Hyannis Port. By nine forty-five p.m., heavy fog had rolled in from the sea, making it impossible to see the fireworks display planned by author George Plimpton, his gift to the newlyweds. "The high point of the reception was when the rockets went up in the clouds and were never seen again," said guest and author John Kenneth Galbraith.

style, they were also gold. This would not do at all—Cecilia's colors were silver and white!

"No problem," said the florist. "We'll run out now and get some silver spray-paint. The chairs will be ready in time for this evening's reception." The mother of the bride was greatly relieved. It was going to be every bit as perfect as she and her daughter had imagined after all.

That evening, Cecilia and Jeff exchanged their vows under a floral arch while the guests sat among the greenery in three hundred silver bamboo chairs. It was indeed a picture-perfect moment, and would have continued to be so—if only the florist had remembered to use quick-drying paint on the chairs.

Instead, he inadvertently provided the guests with a lasting souvenir of Cecilia's painstakingly planned evening. When they got up from their matched chairs to begin dancing, a silver bamboo pattern was neatly imprinted on the backs of their tuxedos and formal gowns.

❤ WEDDING FROM HELL NO. 3 ❤

First, there was a torrential downpour. Marlene and Tom realized that the weather and bad traffic might delay things a bit. But when they arrived ten minutes before their New York wedding ceremony, they found a silent and empty sanctuary. No harpist, no marine honor guard, no guests.

Marlene didn't need this. She was already unnerved from tearing her contact lens the night before and having to cut her own hair because her hairdresser had unexpectedly left town. She was going to have music at her wedding even if she and Tom were the only ones there. Her cousin played the guitar, so she dispatched him home—six blocks away—for his instrument.

Five minutes later, there was a screech of brakes in front of the church. The once deadly quiet church became a flurry of activity. The harpist appeared (followed by the bride's brother, who was enlisted as the harp carrier), the marines rushed in—swords and hats flying— and shortly thereafter, the entire guest list arrived en masse.

The ceremony went smoothly, but then to make things more complicated, Marlene found out that her minister *and* his daughter were planning to attend the reception after all, and the only space in the seating plan was at a table with her rowdiest friends. Then good friends from Texas came through the receiving line and told her that they hadn't realized a meal was being served—they had made plans for dinner.

One problem Marlene had anticipated concerned the dance band. The week before the wedding, she had also been told that the lead singer of her band was too ill to attend, but not to worry—the other musicians would try to sing the moving love songs she'd requested. And so they did—although "sing" might be too generous a word. Actually, they whistled.

And what of the cousin who went for his guitar? By that time, Marlene was in a generous mood. As she and her groom went outdoors to have their pictures taken from the waist up (they were wearing rain boots), she invited him to play at the reception.

CHAPTER 4

You Don't Look So Hot . . .

Imagine your wedding day. As you slip out of bed, you feel radiant, composed, alive with energy. You glance in the mirror . . . flawless skin, glossy hair, sparkling eyes—a true bridal beauty.

—From *BRIDE'S* magazine

❤ ❤ ❤

In Sickness and in Health

The church and reception were decorated; the wedding gown, worn thirty years earlier by the bride's mother, was cleaned and pressed; and three hundred guests were in town for Claire and Todd's wedding in Illinois.

Family and out-of-town guests were now waiting for the bridal party to arrive at the restaurant where the postrehearsal dinner was being held. Just when everyone was beginning to wonder what could possibly take a rehearsal so long, members of the bridal party appeared. The dinner, they announced, wasn't postrehearsal—it was post-wedding. The couple had just been married!

Claire, it turned out, had been feeling ill for several days. At first, her family had chalked it up to pre-wedding jitters, but by the night of the rehearsal, the bride was in such pain that her mother recognized that her daughter was having an appendicitis attack. The minister agreed to marry the couple at the rehearsal, which was photographed and videotaped. Then Claire was taken to the hospital for an immediate appendectomy. It was too late to contact all of the guests, so the groom, who had spent all night at the bride's side, decided to go ahead with the reception as planned. The family rented a large TV to play the impromptu wedding videotape for the shocked wedding guests who arrived the next day.

After the reception, the bridal party, groom, and musicians visited the bride in the hospital, bearing balloons, flowers, wedding cards, and the top layer of the wedding cake. In keeping with the spirit of the occasion, the bride wore a peach negligee to match the bridesmaids' dresses. A strategically placed bridesmaid's fan concealed the medical equipment for the postreception bedside photos. Claire and Todd cut the cake to enthusiastic applause, and then a brother-in-law serenaded the newlyweds with an original ballad composed for the wedding.

❤ ❤ ❤

You try to anticipate everything in a wedding, but Beth and Phil of Kentucky didn't think they'd have to worry that Beth's six-foot-plus, two-hundred-pound brother would faint at the altar. "Right after we said our vows, he fell on a tall, thin groomsman next to him," says Beth. "Then he was pushed into the arms of our five-foot, five-inch best man!"

As four hundred guests watched, the strapping but unconscious groomsman was dragged out of the sanctuary by several ushers, his legs trailing down the aisle after him. Recalls the bride, laughing, "I thought he was dead! And I couldn't *believe* he would die at my wedding!"

Her brother must have unconsciously read her thoughts. His first words upon reviving: "My sister is gonna kill me!"

❤ ❤ ❤

Lloyd knew that his bride, Maureen, wasn't the type to leave him standing at the altar. But he had been waiting there twenty minutes, the vocalist in the Kentucky church was singing "You Are So Beautiful" for what seemed like the millionth time, and the congregation was growing restless.

Then the minister, who was also a paramedic, appeared and told the groom that Maureen was very sick. In fact, at that moment, she was upstairs in the church nursery, swaddled in blankets, gripped by a viral infection that had her retching violently. Each time she tried to put her dress on, she collapsed in a cold sweat.

The groom's first reaction was to postpone the wedding. But the minister explained that they had already filled out the marriage license and according to state law, the wedding had to be that day. If it wasn't, the couple would have to refile for a license and repay the fees.

"This wedding's expensive enough; we're not going to do it again," Lloyd decided.

The minister addressed the worried and whispering guests. "Maureen's very sick and needs her rest," he said. "So we're going to have the reception first to give her time to recuperate."

Lloyd went to the reception, cut his own cake, and toasted his bride. While his guests danced, he went back upstairs to the nursery. In a one-minute ceremony, he exchanged vows and rings with the barely conscious Maureen, who was stretched out on the floor with an oxygen mask on her face. When the minister asked the groom if he wanted to kiss the bride, he politely declined.

An ambulance arrived to take Maureen to the hospital, where the couple spent their first days of married life. The staff helped boost their spirits considerably, hanging a HONEYMOON SUITE sign on the hospital-room door, and carrying in the wedding gifts on a stretcher.

❤ ❤ ❤

When Debra's brother informed her and her groom that he had a sore throat and might have trouble singing at their wedding, they thought it was the worst thing that could happen to them.

They were wrong.

Debra and Billy had completed their wedding vows and her brother was halfway through the hymn when they heard a crash. Debra thought a piano had fallen over, but in fact it was a groomsman who had toppled after fainting, hitting his head on a pew.

The ceremony was quickly concluded and an ambulance sent for, while everyone stood around feeling slightly useless—except for one of Billy's relatives, who announced she was a faith healer, and began massaging the fallen groomsman's temples, chanting prayers for his recovery.

The ambulance arrived, bringing along an unexpected

surprise. The ambulance driver turned out to be the same woman who had made the headpieces for the wedding party, and while she was sorry for the accident, she told the now-overwrought bride and groom that she was grateful to have the chance to see her handiwork on display, rather than having to wait until the photographs were in.

The injured man was rushed to the hospital, had his head stitched up, and returned to the reception. Now it was his wife's turn: a diabetic who had traveled with him to the hospital and back in perfect form, she went into insulin shock. "We had to pump orange juice into her," recalls the bride. And then she was all right. "I'm glad *someone* was!"

❤ ❤ ❤

Jane had spent more than two years planning every detail of her Illinois ceremony and reception. She had provided for every contingency—except chicken pox. Two weeks before the wedding date, the flower girl broke out in spots.

Jane, her groom, Tom, and the rest of the bridal party searched their memories, but no one could recall whether or not the couple had been exposed to chicken pox as children. Two days before the wedding, Jane didn't need to wonder anymore. Telltale signs broke out all over her face.

A postponement would have broken Jane's heart, and refunds were out of the question anyway. The two families decided to go ahead with the wedding, spots and

WEDDING PORTRAIT
The Nuptials of Alice Lee Roosevelt

♥ ♥ ♥

Alice Lee Roosevelt's relationship with her step-mother, Edith, had always been thorny. And on the day of Alice's White House wedding on February 17, 1906, to Congressman Nicholas Longworth from Ohio, it was no better.

Alice was known to be stubborn, and insisted on a high pompadour hairdo, with an enormous hair-piece of orange blossoms and copious veiling. Edith knew it would be a problem. Sure enough, while Alice struggled to effect this hairstyle, government dignitaries and their wives, including members of the Senate, Supreme Court, and the diplomatic corps, were kept waiting in a packed room with closed windows where the temperature quickly rose.

Fifteen minutes before the ceremony was sched-uled to start, guests had already started pushing and straining to see the altar. One woman actually fainted and had to be carried from the room. The windows were opened and the stricken woman returned.

Once the reception was over and the couple were ready to depart, Edith reportedly said to Alice, "I want you to know that I'm glad to see you go. You've never been anything but trouble."

all. Jane wore thick foundation on her face and back, and the photographer cleverly used filters to soften the spots—and avoided close-ups.

The subterfuge worked, and Jane's dream of sharing her life with Tom came true. One of the first things she shared with him was the chicken pox—two days after the ceremony, Tom's face was a sea of spots, and the honeymoon had to be temporarily postponed.

Beauty Blunders

Rachel's waist-length brownish-blond hair was her pride and joy. She had been growing it for eighteen years, and couldn't imagine herself without her crowning glory. For her wedding day, she planned to have it highlighted and pinned up in an elegant Victorian bun.

Since Rachel had heard horror stories of other brides who had gone to the beauty parlor too close to their wedding day, she scheduled an appointment at her regular New Jersey hair salon more than two weeks before the ceremony—close enough so that the highlights would still look fresh on her wedding day, far enough in advance so that if anything should go wrong, there would be enough time to fix it.

It wasn't Rachel's first experience with highlighting, so she thought it was strange when the procedure seemed to take longer than usual. Something else was strange as well—the hairdresser was using foil instead of a cap to highlight her roots.

When the foil was removed thirty minutes later, *strange* turned out to be a hardly adequate description of what Rachel saw. Her lustrous, long hair was now streaked in platinum and orange!

She found out that the hairdresser had been employed

by the salon for just three weeks, and had also violated state law by coloring Rachel's hair without the direct supervision of someone with at least three years of cosmetology experience.

WEDDING PORTRAIT
Ernest Hemingway Weds Hadley Richardson

❤ ❤ ❤

Hadley Richardson of Saint Louis was marrying a man eight years her junior on September 3, 1921. Perhaps it was ambivalence about the marriage that caused her to leave the bridesmaid's hat on the train en route to her wedding to Ernest Hemingway at his family's summer home in Horton Bay, Wisconsin. Her own choice of headpiece was a touchy subject. The opinionated Hemingway had insisted that a veil would be too dressy; Hadley hoped to wear one.

After her arrival, the bride wanted to relax, and decided to go for a swim, forgetting about her thick hair and the closeness of the approaching wedding hour. As a result, she got to wear her veil and a wreath of flowers—out of necessity. It hid her damp hair!

Too shocked to be furious, Rachel's only concern was to restore her hair to its original color—or close to it. The beauticians swarmed over her, pouring on toners, drabbers, and shades of blond. Five-and-a-half hours later, Rachel's hair was no longer orange and white. It was greenish-black.

That night, huge clumps of her hair began to fall out. The next day, Rachel sadly realized that it was time for drastic action. She went to another salon and had her hair cut.

"Eighteen years to grow it and it was gone in ten minutes," she lamented. "Two weeks before my wedding and I have a haircut like a little boy." Rachel's fiancé gallantly told her that it didn't matter, he loved her no matter what. And the wedding took place. Still, he said mournfully, it was a bit hard to take when "this beautiful woman with long hair goes out and comes back looking like Little Bo Peep."

The couple have filed a complaint with the state's board of cosmetology, which is studying the case.

❤ ❤ ❤

The day before her California wedding, Wendy was able to convince a beautician, against her better judgment, to give her an electrolysis treatment on her upper lip. When she awoke on her wedding morning, she looked in the mirror and saw her upper lip swollen well beyond "bee stung" size.

Wendy first considered burying her sorrow in tranquilizers, but instead spent the day applying ice packs to the swollen area. Her diligence paid off. By the time she began to get ready for her evening wedding, her upper lip—though still sensitive—was almost back to its normal size.

Accidents Will Happen

The disc jockey went all out for the wedding reception in New York. He had a bubble-generating machine and laser show to accompany the fifties and sixties music, and the tables emptied with every new song. When he turned on his fog machine, the dancers went wild and formed a conga line.

But in addition to blowing smoke, the fog machine also created long slicks of oil on the ballroom floor. As the conga line wound its way around the room for the third time, Sara, a bridesmaid, slipped, in the excitement. Amid all of the fog, no one realized she went down until the DJ played "Smoke Gets in Your Eyes."

Frivolity pretty much came to a halt when the ambulance arrived to take her to the hospital. Sara was pretty badly bruised and had a broken arm to boot. Not wanting to abandon their fallen maid of honor, the bride and groom later came to visit, sweeping into the emergency room in full bridal regalia—and evoking a round of applause from the ER staff.

❤ ❤ ❤

Rick went skiing three weeks before his February wedding to Ann. He came back a different man. From his big toe up to the middle of his calf there was a fresh white plaster cast, supporting a broken ankle.

The groom was depressed. How could he walk down the aisle? Or dance at his wedding? It would look pretty pathetic, he said.

Ann and her mother decided to make Rick feel less conspicuous. Unbeknownst to him, they had casts put on their legs, too. On the day of the wedding they both limped down the aisle after the groom, to the delighted laughter of family and friends.

❤ ❤ ❤

The newlyweds were all revved up after their Fourth of July wedding in a park in South Carolina. Planning to spend their wedding night at a Grateful Dead concert, Elizabeth and Ron hopped onto his motorcycle, the bride still wearing her cream-colored wedding gown.

But in making her dramatic exit, the bride neglected to sweep up the long train and keep it safely away from the back wheel. The fabric got caught in the spokes and dragged her under the bike. Paramedics at the scene had to shred the fabric to free her. The bride spent her wedding night—and her first newlywed weeks—in the hospital, recovering from a concussion and a broken pelvis.

❤ ❤ ❤

Tom was truly looking forward to being best man at his older brother John's New York wedding. For the first time in a long time, the entire extended family would be together—even the brothers' elderly aunt, who was driving up from Florida with their grandfather.

But at the reception, shortly after Tom's toast to his brother, things began to go awry. The band was in full swing when Tom's aunt went out on the dance floor. Suddenly, she slipped and fell flat on the floor. Although other guests tried to help her up, she could not move. The music had to stop—it was no competition for the aunt's moans of pain.

The thoughtful best man didn't want other family members to miss John's wedding, so he volunteered to accompany his aunt to the emergency room—where he spent the rest of the evening, in his elegant tuxedo.

❤ ❤ ❤

Natalie was helping her brother roll up a hose outside her parents' home the day before her wedding, when the hose snapped back and hit her smack in the face. Although she was more stunned than hurt, a nasty-looking black-and-blue mark developed right above her eye in a matter of hours.

Fearing that the guests would be confused by a bride who looked like she had spent the night before her wedding in a street brawl, Natalie deployed an entire tin of eye shadow to duplicate the now darkened lid on her other eye. She also used a double dose of blush, hoping extra rosy cheeks would provide a good distraction.

It worked with at least one person: the groom told Natalie that she looked particularly glamorous that day.

❤ WEDDING FROM HELL NO. 4 ❤

Ruth and Ben had planned a sunset wedding by the sea in Israel, the groom's place of birth. But the rabbi arrived two hours late. As darkness fell, the hotel turned on its outdoor lights so the festivities could proceed. When the rabbi finally arrived, he first offered a thousand explanations for the delay. Then, he indicated that the procession could begin.

Just as it was the bride's turn to start down the aisle, the hotel experienced one of Israel's frequent power outages. Stumbling down the aisle in the unanticipated moonlight, Ruth somehow managed to reach the altar. The rabbi, now without a working microphone, started to shout the service. The lights continued to flicker on and off. At one point they came on precisely at the moment that the videographer was pointing his light directly into the bride's face. She said "I do" in a state of temporary blindness.

Meanwhile a sea of children, all under the age of ten, ran to and fro, buzzing around the huppah. The bride and her groom finally walked back up the aisle slowly, thanks to the assistance of several young train bearers who seemed to think the couple should be going in at least three other directions, and who tugged the bride's train accordingly.

CHAPTER 5

Chapel Nightmares

This is the big moment, one of the richest experiences the two of you will ever share. Like many couples today, you'll want your ceremony to be steeped in tradition, to convey the importance of this step called marriage; but full of personal touches that show the unique quality of your love.

—From *BRIDE'S Book of Etiquette*

❤ ❤ ❤

Ceremony Saboteurs

As the bride and her bridesmaids stepped out of their limousine to enter the church before the wedding in North Carolina, they passed by a drunken woman who was sitting on a low brick wall that surrounded the building. Even in her less-than-sober state, the woman grasped the significance of the moment, and began ranting. "You'll be miserable! He's no damn good! Don't get married, it's hell!" These and other cheering observations stung the entourage hurrying into the church.

But the unwelcome chorus did not end when they closed the door behind them. It was a warm summer day, and since the church had no air-conditioning, the windows were wide open. All during the ceremony, the woman kept up a screaming torrent of curses, epithets, and tales of doom. The officiant bravely proceeded with the ceremony, while the appalled guests strained to hear the altar proceedings.

Finally, four police cars arrived on the scene with sirens blaring. The guests exited the church just in time to see the officers wrestling the woman to the ground and loading her into the backseat of one of their cars—

as she continued to admonish all within earshot of the follies of wedded bliss.

❤ ❤ ❤

To cool off the congregation during Leah and Alan's August New York wedding, the synagogue windows were opened wide to let in a fresh breeze. Halfway through the ceremony, a car cruised up the street and stopped at the corner to wait for the light to change. Its powerful tape deck blared rap music so loud that the wedding service inside the synagogue was drowned out for quite a few minutes. The rabbi and cantor patiently waited their turn, and, at last, the car drove on.

At the reception, the groom thanked his new in-laws for the beautiful wedding and, most of all, for the rap music they had thoughtfully arranged for everyone's entertainment during the ceremony.

❤ ❤ ❤

Just as Ron and Christine began to exchange their vows, the photographer decided to make sure he had one picture that included every detail of the precious moment. He took a step backward from the altar to get a wider perspective, and landed directly on the toe of Ron's great-grandmother, who was sitting in the front pew.

She responded with a low moan that escalated rapidly—much like a cow mooing, thought the guests, as the bovine moans of pain reverberated, thanks to the excellent acoustics of the church. So rattled was Ron by

WEDDING PORTRAIT
Franklin Roosevelt Weds

♥ ♥ ♥

In retrospect, March 17, 1905, Saint Patrick's Day, probably was not the best choice for a wedding date. But Eleanor and Franklin Roosevelt wanted then-president Theodore Roosevelt (uncle of the groom) to give the bride away, and he would be in New York City that day to make a speech.

The wedding was held in the elegant side-by-side homes of Eleanor's relatives at Six East Sixty-sixth Street, just off Fifth Avenue. Just as some of the most prestigious names on the *Social Register*—Vanderbilt, Van Rensselaer, Mortimer, and Sloane—were making their way to the wedding, the Saint Patrick's Day parade was heading down Fifth Avenue. Eleanor, resplendent in her gown, and bejeweled with a collar of pearls, a diamond bowknot and diamond crescent fastening her veil, was escorted down the staircase by the President.

Slowly but surely, the boisterous strains of "The Wearin' o' the Green" approached and overrode the stately "Wedding March." Curious onlookers, who broke through police cordons in hopes of seeing the President, grew noisy and restless. Guests were hard-pressed to hear any of the wedding music, or the thoughtfully chosen words of The Reverend Endicott Peabody, friend of Eleanor and Franklin, who was performing the ceremony.

the "oo-oo-oo-oo-OO-OO-OO!!" rising up from the front pew that he said "I do" too soon.

Like the couple's exchange of vows, this was too precious a moment to forget. And since it couldn't be captured on film, Ron and Christine's guests did the next best thing at the reception—they reenacted it. Throughout the party, pairs of friends could be seen stepping on each other, then responding with a resounding "Moo-oo-oo-oo."

♥ ♥ ♥

The organ in the New York City church began to play the opening chords of the "Wedding March." Guests craned their necks toward the vestibule. But instead of seeing the wedding party walk down the aisle, they saw the father of the bride and the bride running out the door.

The brouhaha was over the father of the bride's car, which was being towed away from its parking spot in front of the church. Dad, a small-town sheriff, ran down the steps and tried to argue his way out of the ticket and towing. Kathy, the bride, ran out to help her father. Other members of the bride's family joined the fracas, pleading, cajoling, and cursing. Since it was summer, the church doors had been opened to let in a warm breeze, allowing the guests to hear every word—including some indelicate ones—from the confrontation. Meanwhile, as the processional music wafted into the street, the groom and the best man remained frozen in front of the church until the car was towed away.

That evening, the newlyweds lent Kathy's father

money from their gift envelopes so he could retrieve his car. Just one more expense added to the tab of doing wedding business in New York City, he grumbled.

♥ ♥ ♥

What was the most nerve-racking part of Ann's wedding? It wasn't the torrential rain, the late limousine,

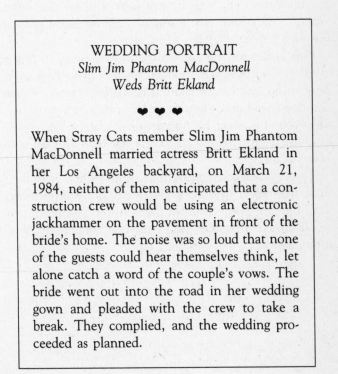

WEDDING PORTRAIT
Slim Jim Phantom MacDonnell
Weds Britt Ekland

♥ ♥ ♥

When Stray Cats member Slim Jim Phantom MacDonnell married actress Britt Ekland in her Los Angeles backyard, on March 21, 1984, neither of them anticipated that a construction crew would be using an electronic jackhammer on the pavement in front of the bride's home. The noise was so loud that none of the guests could hear themselves think, let alone catch a word of the couple's vows. The bride went out into the road in her wedding gown and pleaded with the crew to take a break. They complied, and the wedding proceeded as planned.

the traffic jam, or the missing boutonniere. It wasn't the groom's insistence on placing his bride's ring on the wrong finger. It wasn't even the arrival of the wrong cake—decorated with tacky plastic swans.

No, the worst moment was captured on video. Just as she completed her walk down the seemingly endless aisle and the service began, sirens sounded loudly from the firehouse across the street. The priest vainly tried to outshout the wail, "but he just looked like a silent-film actor," says Ann. "Not a sound could be heard coming out of his mouth!"

Finally he gave up and waited for the sirens to cease. As they died down, he opened his mouth to start over, only to be met by the blaring sirens once more. Again the noise died down and again the priest began the service—but this time he was drowned out by fire engine after fire engine roaring out of the station house, all with horns blaring.

The bride couldn't make up her mind whether to faint from frustration or simply give up and try on another day. But the priest relieved the tension by announcing to all present that the bride must have previously jilted a fireman!

Little Rascals

Maggie thought that Joy, the five-year-old sister of her fiancé, Chester, would make an adorable flower girl at their New York wedding. And she was right. Joy walked slowly down the aisle, being careful not to strew too many rose petals in one place, and smiled a big smile. The guests were charmed. When Joy reached the altar, however, she turned around and began to walk back up the aisle, straight toward the wedding party who had been following her. She was picking up rose petals as she went!

Trying to prevent a major collision on the aisle, one of the guests grabbed her arm to stop her. "Come and sit down, Joy," the guest coaxed. "You don't need to do that."

"No!" squealed the child, her clear voice resounding throughout the church. "My mommy taught me that if you make a pigsty, you clean it up. And I just made an awful mess!"

❤ ❤ ❤

David's aunt thought that her four-year-old nephew would better perform his duties as ring bearer if he received a present before the ceremony to take his mind off the crowd. It worked wonderfully—except that no amount of cajoling could get him to then let go of his aunt's present. When it came time to march down the aisle, the solemn little gentleman performed wonderfully—clutching not only the ring pillow, but also a container of Superman bubble bath.

♥ ♥ ♥

Janet and Tom loved children. They especially loved the three-year-old daughter of their usher Jim. So they asked her to be a flower girl in their church wedding in Alabama.

After escorting a bridesmaid down the aisle, Jim took his place at the altar and proudly watched his daughter make her walk, throwing her flower petals with abandon. Suddenly, halfway down the aisle, she froze. She had realized that everyone was staring at her!

Following her, the bride stopped cold. In fact, everyone seemed to be stuck on freeze frame—except the organist, who dutifully continued playing the "Wedding March."

Jim realized that there was only one way to start the action rolling. He left his place at the front of the church, went down the aisle, and picked up his daughter. Safe in her father's arms, she remembered her job and began to throw petals again. As if someone had turned off the pause button on a VCR, the bride proceeded down the aisle to the altar.

❤ ❤ ❤

Karen and Robert's wedding service was a reverent and moving occasion—until the couple each took a candle and lit a third as a symbol of their union. At that moment, the three-year-old ring bearer cheerfully launched into a rendition of "Happy Birthday."

❤ ❤ ❤

The flower girl for Carolyn and Brad's wedding arrived at the Indiana church shortly before the ceremony, perfectly groomed in a beautiful new dress. But as she entered the waiting area, she inadvertently passed too close to a standing fan. The dress was instantaneously sucked into the whirling blades, ripping off the bottom half.

The girl was frightened but unharmed. Although the ceremony was due to start any minute, no one behind the scenes had a needle and thread. The resourceful wedding consultant salvaged the dress by taping the hem on the inside. The bride breathed a sigh of relief, and the ceremony proceeded as planned.

It wasn't until the mended flower girl had started on her adorable way down the aisle that it became very apparent she needed a slip. Row by row, the wedding guests chuckled as they caught a glimpse of the little girl's Wonder Woman underwear—its red, white, and blue stars and stripes boldly showing through her pale pink dress.

❤ ❤ ❤

On her wedding day in New York, Madeline was all set to start down the aisle to meet Grant, her groom, when their four-year-old flower girl decided she wasn't going to be making the trip. Nothing could persuade the child to go down the aisle.

The five-year-old ring bearer decided that it was his duty to drag the little girl down the aisle. The struggling pair reached the halfway point when the bullheaded little girl decided she'd had enough. Whirling around, she bit the ring bearer on the arm with all her might. One hundred fifty guests gasped, then waited in suspense for an all-out junior wrestling match to ensue.

The children eyed each other for a moment, and then the little girl broke out in a big smile. Ever the little gentleman, the ring bearer decided that discretion was indeed the better part of valor, and continued down the aisle with his now strangely satisfied partner, rubbing his wounded arm the rest of the way.

Errant Officiants

A rabbi and a priest were to perform a garden wedding ceremony together at a hall in New Jersey. But when the priest didn't show up, one of the waiters came over to the banquet manager. "I'm in the seminary," he said. "I can do this ceremony."

With the blessing of the relieved couple, he somehow managed to pull together the correct attire, co-officiate, and join the receiving line.

It was a busy day at the hall, and several other weddings were underway. Those still offering their good wishes in the receiving line were startled when the maître d' approached the priest and asked, "Excuse me, Father. Would you mind going to the Birch Garden to set up the buffet table?"

❤ ❤ ❤

The invitations for Audrey and Chet's wedding asked guests to be at a synagogue in New York at six-thirty p.m. The ceremony was to begin at seven-thirty p.m., but the time came and went with no rabbi. "The guests didn't notice anything unusual," recalls Audrey. "They just kept eating from the smorgasbord that had been planned for before the ceremony."

The rabbi eventually showed up, and Audrey and her betrothed said their vows at eight p.m. "But he really threw the timing off," she says. "We didn't enter the dining room until nine p.m., and because the next day was a workday, a lot of people started leaving during dessert. Then we had to pay overtime to the caterer and the band—three thousand dollars extra!"

"At least our mission—getting married—was accomplished," she sighs.

❤ ❤ ❤

Sue and her groom, David, were getting married in the bride's hometown in Maryland. The night before the ceremony, the wedding party gathered with the rabbi for a quick rehearsal. Having spent too much time waiting for weddings that started late, the rabbi sternly reminded everyone that tomorrow's event would start at seven-thirty p.m.—sharp.

But David's mother sensed disaster and told the rabbi that her friends always arrived at a wedding at least a half an hour after it was to start—because the weddings *never* started on time. The rabbi was unmoved. "Well, this one will, and they're going to miss a lot of the ceremony."

The following day, true to form, the friends of the groom's mother were nowhere to be seen when seven-thirty approached. She was distraught that her dear friends might miss her son's wedding—until a brilliant scheme dawned on her. She secretly returned to her hotel room across the street. I'll hide out here until eight p.m., she thought. If they can't find me, Sue and David will surely delay the ceremony.

Not fooled one bit by this ruse, the rabbi sent a messenger over to the mother's hotel room. "If you're not there in ten minutes," shouted the messenger outside the door, "they're starting the ceremony without you!"

It was a fair deal—she was no match for a savvy man of God. The groom's mother sighed, picked up her purse, and came out of hiding.

❤ ❤ ❤

Katy was American, her groom, Juan, was Peruvian, and they were getting married at city hall in a city in Belgium. It should have been a ten-minute ceremony at most, but the unusual multinational combination seemed to inspire the local officiant, who turned out to be the mayor. As the couple stood stunned, he launched into a lengthy oration, using the union of the bride and groom as an extended metaphor for the importance of developed and underdeveloped nations working together for world peace.

Only when he had utterly exhausted his global-literary-economic conceit did he pronounce Katy and Juan man and wife—at which point, the building's recorded music system began to play "Don't Cry for Me, Argentina."

❤ ❤ ❤

Evelyn knew that because her rabbi was from Maryland, he wouldn't be able to sign the marriage license after the wedding in New York. She assumed that the synagogue's cantor would be able to tie up any legal loose ends.

But on the day of the wedding, Evelyn and Robbie discovered that it was the cantor's son who would be performing at their wedding—and he wasn't licensed by the state, either.

The couple decided they weren't going to let anything stop them—not even the law. They went through with the ceremony, reception, and even the honeymoon. When they came back, they had a private ceremony with the New York synagogue's rabbi, who signed the piece of paper. Evelyn and Robbie's guests never suspected that they had attended an extrajudicial event.

❤ ❤ ❤

The bride and groom were ready to begin the rest of their lives together. There was just one hitch—no one had shown up to pronounce them man and wife.

With the appointed time for the New York ceremony long past, and with guests getting ever restless, relatives ran out into the streets to local churches to recruit another man of the cloth—just about any cloth would do at this point. Finally, a likely candidate was spotted.

There was just one problem: the clergyman was just returning from a convention, and he didn't have his prayer book. Nonetheless, he valiantly performed the ceremony from memory—with a few lapses here and there.

❤ ❤ ❤

WEDDING PORTRAIT
Hugh Hefner Weds Kimberly Conrad

❤ ❤ ❤

Even on the wedding day, June 1, 1989, guests and friends of the couple found it hard to believe that the eternal swinger, *Playboy* guru and founder Hugh Hefner, then 63, was really going to marry former Playmate of the Year Kimberly Conrad, then 26. The minister who officiated at the nondenominational California ceremony at the Playboy mansion found the event incredible, too. Immediately after Hef said "I do," the Reverend Charles Ara asked the audience at large, "You heard him say that? Everybody out there—he said it!"

Mary and Charles wanted a traditional Buddhist wedding ceremony, and made arrangements with the minister in their local temple to conduct the services.

The minister became seriously ill a month before the wedding, but thought he would be well by the wedding date. A week before the ceremony, however, he became ill again. Mary and Charles had to find someone else who could not only perform a Buddhist ceremony, but who also would be available in seven days.

Finally a new officiant was found, but he was not available for the date of the wedding. So the bride and groom decided to change the date. But it meant relocating to a site with room for only fifteen—and they had invited two hundred guests! Mary had to contact everyone and break the news that although they were welcome at the reception, they would not be able to witness the wedding ceremony.

The couple then discovered that the man who would marry them was a Buddhist monk, not a minister. He was authorized to perform the Buddhist ritual, but was not authorized by the state to sign the marriage license. Mary and Charles had to find yet another minister (having exhausted the supply of Buddhists, they opted for one of a different faith) to witness the ceremony and sign the certificate.

Even the honeymoon was not spared. Changing the wedding date forced the couple to cancel their wedding trip, because leaving after the new date would have conflicted with Mary's job teaching school. As of this writing, four years later, they still haven't gotten away—but they're planning to, for their fifth anniversary!

Uninvited Guests

Ted and Iris wanted a very simple outdoor ceremony. So, on a pristine mountain golf course in Colorado, a party of four—the bride, the groom, the best man, and a municipal court judge—gathered to hear the couple pledge their vows.

As it turned out, there was one uninvited guest. Just after the couple were pronounced husband and wife, a three-hundred-pound black bear emerged from the neighboring woods and ambled over to them. As the bridal party stood petrified with fear, the animal slo-o-o-wly sniffed each one of them from head to toe. Next, it gently nipped at the quaking groom's hand in a kind of rough handshake, and then stood on its hind legs and pounded on the wedding car. Having thus proffered his congratulations, the four-legged intruder ambled back into the woods.

❤ ❤ ❤

Annemarie wanted to be surrounded by nature at her summer evening garden wedding in New York. She never expected, however, that the softly flickering candles and lights would attract hundreds of tiny insects to the ceremony. Finding herself trapped inside a veil filled with little uninvited guests, she wisely decided to dispense with a headpiece all together.

❤ ❤ ❤

When the consultant arrived at Kathy's home the morning of her wedding, she found the bride hysterical. Her father's car had been stolen (later, it was discovered that he had forgotten where he had parked it). There was no hot water in the house for a shower (the consultant arranged for everyone to take showers at a neighbor's). Those problems solved, it seemed like a home wedding, under a tent in the bride's backyard, would be just fine. But Heinrich had other plans.

Heinrich was a German shepherd that belonged, not coincidentally, to Kathy's German aunts, who had flown all the way to New York for the wedding. Although the aunts spoke only German, the wedding consultant tried as best she could to urge them to keep the dog shut up in a room—away from the wedding guests.

But either through a failure to communicate or sheer canine wiliness, Heinrich escaped and ran into the midst of the reception. Galloping across the tent, he knocked over an elderly lady, who had to be taken by the rescue squad to the hospital.

Certain that they were a sitting target for the predatory pooch, the band decided it was a good time for a break. After much pleading and cajoling from the consultant, the musicians got back into position so the party could carry on.

Heinrich was evicted before he could catch the bouquet.

❤ ❤ ❤

Sensing that a wedding was taking place (and intuiting, as well, that she was dressed appropriately), a pure-white cat entered the July ceremony in a New York church through an open front door, strolled up the aisle, squeezed between the bridal couple standing at the altar, and sat down near the feet of the officiating pastor.

Guests tried to muffle their laughter, but the minister, who was legally blind, seemed not to notice the sudden feline addition to the bridal party. The seven-year-old ring bearer, who had been bored with all the goings on, now made it absolutely clear that he wanted to play with the cat. As the groom attempted to restrain the ring bearer, the cat began to prowl about the altar, riveting the attention of everyone but the still-oblivious clergyman.

The cat settled in for a nap on the altar steps—a position that would surely serve to trip the shortsighted minister and send him tumbling when he descended at the close of the ceremony. A fast-thinking usher rushed forward and whisked the cat away just as the minister began his move.

The cat was deposited on the steps outside the church, but the imperious puss would not stay put. She reentered the building and made it halfway down the aisle before the wedding coordinator grabbed her, took her outside again, and plopped her on the steps with a stern warning.

This time, the cat chose to remain outside until the ceremony was over. After all, now she was in purr-fect position for the receiving line.

Objections and Other "Altarcations"

After a one-hour mass, the priest addressed the congregation. Did anyone have any objections to the marriage taking place?

The usual second of silence passed, and then the bride cleared her throat. "Yes, I object," Marianne said clearly. Turning to the groom, she added, "And I object to your sleeping with my maid of honor."

Then Marianne took a bridesmaid's hand, made an about-face, and walked defiantly down the aisle and out of the church, followed by the entire bridal party (minus the maid of honor and the groom). Everyone was invited to the reception to celebrate the bride's close call.

♥ ♥ ♥

As the bride walked down the aisle, her soon-to-be mother-in-law rose and yelled, "He's making the biggest mistake of his life!" The bride's cheeks flushed, but still she continued resolutely toward the altar.

The vows were exchanged, and the couple recessed

up the aisle together. "They'll be divorced in six months!" the groom's mother cried out.

The resigned bride explains, "We're different religions. On holidays, she calls and tells my husband they expect him, but I'm not invited; leave me in the car! She even set up a bank account for Mitchell to use after he divorces me! He told them, 'Accept my wife or lose me.' We have nothing to do with his parents now.

"It's not just me she has a problem with," adds the bride. "When my husband's younger brother married, she followed him down the aisle. Holding on to the back of his tuxedo, she shouted, 'You can still get out of this!'"

❤ ❤ ❤

The minister reached the point in the marriage ceremony where he stated, "If anyone knows any reason why this wedding should not take place, speak now or forever hold your peace." Dramatically, a man rose up from a back pew, strode up the aisle to the altar, and peered into the faces of the bride and groom. "Oops!" he exclaimed. "Wrong couple!" He then strode back down the aisle and out of the church.

❤ ❤ ❤

The night before her wedding, a Texas bride drove over to her fiancé's house. Surprised to see her maid of honor's car in front, she let herself in the front door with her key. There, she quietly walked in on her groom-to-be—in bed with her best friend!

Amazingly composed, she walked directly out of the house, and planned the perfect revenge. Wedding-day plans proceeded on schedule. She had her hair done, and drove with her family in the limousine to the large cathedral where the ceremony would take place. The six ushers seated hundreds of guests. The mothers were seated. The aisle runner was unrolled. Then the bride, in a formal gown with a cathedral train, was escorted down the aisle by her father.

At the altar, when the priest asked, "If anyone knows any reason why this wedding should not take place, speak now or forever hold your peace," the bride clearly spoke up. "Last night, the maid of honor slept with the groom, and this wedding will *not* take place!" she declared. She then turned abruptly, train whipping around behind, strode back down the aisle and out of the church, leaving her stunned guests, groom, and former best friend behind.

❤ ❤ ❤

At the point when the priest asked if there was anyone present who objects to the couple being joined in holy matrimony, to everyone's horror, a young man stood up and declared that the wedding should not be allowed.

The ceremony was stopped while the bride, groom, priest, and young man went into the office to discuss the matter. It turned out that the gentleman was a spurned ex-lover of the bride, and as this was not a reasonable objection in anyone's opinion (except the jiltee's), the wedding continued—without any other objections.

❤ ❤ ❤

Eric's parents thought he was too young to marry Jean, his high-school sweetheart. He was sure once they got to the altar, everyone would come around, but when the minister asked, "Can anyone show just cause why these two should not be married?" his mother rose. "Eric," she announced loudly, "if you back out now, we will sign over the deed of the summer house to you and allocate a sizable income as well!"

But true love conquers even money and desirable real estate—the groom opted to continue with the ceremony as planned.

♥ WEDDING FROM HELL NO. 5 ♥

Before Pamela's mother died, she made a last request: She wanted her only child to have a beautiful wedding.

So when his daughter announced her intention to marry Edward, Pamela's father decided to spare no cost. He put all the decisions into the hands of the caterer, who was planning the wedding at a New York City synagogue.

Everything that could possibly go wrong *did*.

The morning of her wedding, the bride went to pick up her dress. With the gown and veil in the back of her car, the bride got back onto the expressway and hit bumper-to-bumper traffic. Like any New Yorker in a hurry, she decided to pick up time by driving on the shoulder. When a policeman stopped her, Pamela explained that it was her wedding day. The officer pulled his car in front of hers, put his siren on, and escorted her through traffic, directly to her house. It was the only nice thing that was to happen for the rest of the day.

Ready at last for the drive to the synagogue, the bride and her attendants stepped into their limousine. It would have been a relaxed, elegant drive if the driver had been able to turn off the heater in the car. Instead, the bride and all of the maids pulled up to the synagogue with their freshly coiffed heads hanging out the window.

The rabbi arrived very late. The cantor never arrived.

Once the ceremony was underway, Edward noticed that his brother, a member of the wedding party, seemed to be leaning against a pole of the huppah. It was a keen observation—a few moments later, the brother passed out. The best man grabbed the spare pole, and guests helped the usher out of the sanctuary.

At the reception, there were not enough chairs for the guests. While everyone watched, more were brought up from downstairs and set up noisily in the ballroom. And only one person from the original band they had contracted with showed up. The lead singer had strep throat, and another person had been in a car accident, or so they were told.

The food was unusually slow in being served. Finally, the caterer admitted to the bride that things were behind schedule because he and his staff had just finished serving a large bar mitzvah held in the same room. Waiters started serving the main course, fish, at eight p.m. Guests trying to cut the filet found it was frozen solid in the center. When one of the guests complained, the caterer impatiently replied, "This is the second party I've done today. You want *food*?" That's when the fistfight broke out. It just so happened it was during the bride's dance with her father. By midnight, most guests still hadn't eaten.

Still, the hungry relatives weren't going to let a wedding go by without a rousing rendition of the horah. As is traditional, the parents were lifted up on chairs. The groom's father was playfully tossed into the air—and right onto the floor. (He wasn't hurt.)

At the end of the reception, the caterer had the nerve to ask the bride's father for one hour of overtime pay. The slow and surly service, the frozen fish, the fact that the promised Viennese dessert table never materialized—it was too much for the father of the bride. Pamela's father grabbed the caterer by the collar of his shirt and threw him down the steps of the synagogue.

❤ CHAPTER 6 ❤

Battling the Elements

♥ ♥ ♥

Unpredictable weather throws a snag into many a wedding. . . . Even though you've planned your reception in a museum garden, or a horse-and-carriage getaway, no one can guarantee you cloudless blue skies.

From *BRIDE'S Book of Etiquette*

♥ ♥ ♥

Rain on the Parade

It looked like Sara and Sam's botanical garden wedding would have to move indoors. The rain had fallen steadily over New York the whole week before, and workmen hadn't even been able to install the tent for the reception.

But the wedding day dawned and the sun was finally shining. A good omen, everyone thought—let's get that tent up and go!

So the tent was duly set up, and a wooden platform was constructed to serve as the dance floor and keep the band's equipment dry.

Unfortunately, there was no way to protect guests from the general muddiness of the grounds. All one hundred fifty guests in formal gowns and tuxedos had to slog across the lawn, trailing mud and grass up onto the dance floor. Many of the female guests simply gave up, shed their high heels, and went barefoot. And whatever wasn't on the dance floor—including the tables and chairs—simply sunk into the mire.

Meanwhile, the bride made an interesting discovery: her elaborate gown soaked up mud and water like a natural sponge. Before long, she was stained to the waist. There were no full-length photographs that day. Then the heavens opened up and it began to pour.

The bride remained calm, the guests stoic. The disc jockey played terrific lively music that kept everybody dancing for hours. So what if the dance floor had to be mopped up every fifteen minutes?

❤ ❤ ❤

Adrianna and Ross could not believe their good luck! Just ten hours earlier, Hurricane Gloria had been wreaking rain, wind, and damage on the metropolitan New York area. Yet Sunday morning, the day of their autumn 1985 wedding, dawned clear and crisp. Power had been restored to the New Jersey golf club where their reception was to be held, and all of the fallen branches had been carted away.

Of course, it was muddy for the outdoor ceremony and cocktails. But the dinner was going to be held inside, and the bride and groom were sure that the muck would have no further effect on their perfect evening. As the newlyweds took their seats at the head table, they noticed that all of their guests were expectantly looking toward them. No one would begin the first course, and although the orchestra was playing, no one was on the dance floor.

"Dad, everyone's waiting for the first dance. We have to begin," Adrianna implored her father.

"We're not starting without your mother, sweetie," he replied firmly.

"Mike, do something!" the bride hissed to her brother. "You've got to go get Mom! The last time I saw her, she was heading for the rest room. There are 180 people waiting for her!"

Sometime shortly before eternity ended, the brother of the bride returned with his mother in tow. Oblivious to the waiting ballroom full of guests, she walked—with head erect—to the head table. "I was washing off my shoes," explained the bride's mother matter-of-factly. "Did you notice how muddy it was out there?"

❤ ❤ ❤

At an outdoor New York reception, the tent sprung a leak and water began to drip directly onto the bride's head. The caterer realized that it would be impossible to move the bride to a drier area without interrupting food service and moving many guests and tables.

To salvage the situation, the caterer asked one of the waiters, who also happened to be a model, to stand behind the bride with a Grecian urn in hand—to catch the raindrops. The man, who had classic good looks, assumed a statuesque pose and held the urn for the duration of the first course, till the tent was patched.

❤ ❤ ❤

You can look it up in *The Old Farmer's Almanac*—it doesn't rain in California in September. Still, the wedding consultant was nervous—weather reports had predicted rain.

"Do you want me to order a tent?" she asked Edith

the evening before the wedding. Edith and Mark looked at the sky. The sunset was magnificent. Rain tomorrow? No way. Why spend money on a tent that will just stand empty? The consultant persisted. "I'll split the expenses with you," she suggested. "I'd just like us to be safe."

"No, no, no!" repeated the bride and groom, their two hearts beating as one. "It is absolutely not necessary—just look at the sky!" So against all her better instincts, the consultant gave in. The rehearsal dinner ended happily and the wedding party headed home.

Later that night, the rains—no, make that the *monsoons*—descended with a fury. There was nothing to do but change the wedding plans, including the location, to a place where a tent could be set up.

"Finding a tent man in the middle of the night when every other bride in town was looking for one too was quite an ordeal," recalls the consultant. Finally a tent was located in another town, and the bride called every one of her guests to inform them of the location switch. Knowing there was too much work for her and her assistants to handle alone, the consultant called on her family and personal friends to help move supplies and set up the tent.

Did the guests mind the last-minute switch? Not a bit. In fact, they spent almost as much time marveling at the wedding's organization as they did at the bride's dress.

❤ ❤ ❤

It was on a houseboat that romance had blossomed for the California couple. So when they decided to tie the knot, there was no question as to the setting.

WEDDING PORTRAIT
Marie Antoinette Weds Louis XV

♥ ♥ ♥

Even royal types have trouble with rain. It was raining at Versailles on May 7, 1770, the wedding day of 14-year-old Marie Antoinette to Louis XV of France. The bride wore a white gown of brocade, the groom a suit of gold cloth. It rained so hard that edges of the wedding pavilion kept collapsing under the weight of water, and the ladies-in-waiting were drenched. A magnificent fireworks display planned in celebration had to be canceled.

All of this seemed to have a deleterious effect on the couple—the marriage was not consummated for seven years. Nineteen years later, on July 14, 1789, a revolutionary crowd stormed the Bastille, and three years after that, the monarchy was brought down by the French Revolution. Louis was beheaded in January of 1793, and the following October, Marie was also condemned to death by the Revolutionary Council.

But when their wedding day arrived, it was raining buckets. The minister met with the couple in a nearby house, certain that they would want to change their minds. "Wouldn't you like to have the ceremony in the house?" he asked, using his most persuasive tone of voice.

"No, no, no," they replied. "We met on a houseboat, courted on a houseboat, and we intend to be married on a houseboat."

The downpour continued with no sign of abating. The minister looked outside, and turning to the couple, tried once again. "How about getting married in the church next door? It's nice and dry."

"No," they replied, insisting again on the houseboat.

So the wedding party left the house and traipsed through the rain and mud to where the boat was moored at the bottom of the hill. For a little while they sat inside the boat's cabin, listening to the rain pound on the roof and waiting for it to stop.

It never will, thought the minister. He looked at the bride, dressed in a floor-length burgundy velvet dress, and at the groom, in his freshly pressed business suit, and made a last-ditch attempt. "Why don't we have the ceremony right in here?" he asked.

"No, no, no," the bride and groom firmly responded to his suggestion. "It has to be outside!"

The minister gave up all hope of remaining unsaturated. "Very well, then," he said. "Let's go do it!"

The bridal party headed up to the roof of the houseboat and were married in the pouring rain. Says the minister, dryly, of the day, "Even the martinis were wet."

❤ ❤ ❤

For three days before Joann's outdoor Virginia wedding it rained and rained. But the skies cleared on the important day, and everything would proceed as planned.

Or would it? The organist was awakened at seven a.m. by a phone call from Joann's mother. The music company was refusing to send an organ for an outdoor service so soon after the rain. The organist would have to make do with a neighbor's rickety old upright piano.

Somehow, the piano was maneuvered onto the soggy lawn and the organist managed to quickly find something appropriate in her piano music. But halfway through playing the "Wedding March," the organist began to get a sinking feeling. Her hands seemed to be getting higher and higher. Could the keyboard be levitating? No, the piano bench was sinking—into the soggy ground.

Frantically, she tried gently to push the bench back and stand up to play, but with all four legs of the piano bench sunk in the muck, it fell over with a crash into a tall candelabrum stand, which then tumbled onto a bridesmaid.

The bride burst into tears. Spectators' faces alternated between expressions of horror and hilarity. With the equanimity of which only the clergy are capable, the minister noted that the occurrence would make the wedding all the more memorable for everyone involved.

Up in Smoke

Joey, Michele, and their guests had just begun the main course of their seated wedding reception meal in the medium-sized hall. The band started to play quiet dinner music. Suddenly, the roof caved in on the unsuspecting guests.

The place was on fire! It was chaos: smoke, rubble, the guests being carried out on stretchers. But one person refused to lose his cool—the banquet hall manager, who was heard asking a dazed member of the wedding party, "Would you like us to move you to another room?"

❤ ❤ ❤

Carolyn and Keith searched for a wedding site in Washington, D.C., where they could host both the ceremony and reception. One particular hotel seemed perfect for the occasion.

As the ceremony proceeded, cooks prepared vegetable tempura for the cocktail hour to follow. Smoke from the hot oil set off the smoke detectors, and just as Carolyn and Keith were about to say their vows, a deafening buzz shook the building. Then prerecorded directions were

WEDDING PORTRAIT
Joan Rivers Weds Jimmy Sanger

❤ ❤ ❤

By her own admission, the first wedding of Joan Molinsky Rivers was a mistake. The rabbi who performed it probably has mixed feelings about it, as well. Joan married Jimmy Sanger, a young man she met while working at Bond's stores. At the end of the ceremony in the New York City Park Avenue apartment of Joan's aunt, the rabbi reached through an elaborate arrangement of candles and caught the sleeves of his robe on fire. Bridesmaid Nancy Heath was very impressed. She told Joan that she had never been to a Jewish wedding before and did not realize that the rabbi was sacrificed at the end!

broadcast continuously from the hotel public address system: "You must leave the building immediately! Please go to the nearest exit and leave the building immediately!"

The wedding consultant kept reassuring the uneasy guests that it was just the smoke from the kitchen that had set off the alarms, but their fears certainly weren't assuaged when firemen, required to thoroughly check a building after an alarm goes off, clomped through the beautifully decorated ceremony room in their slickers and big black boots.

The area was deemed safe, and the service continued. Needless to say, "Smoke Gets in Your Eyes" was not among the songs requested at the reception.

❤ ❤ ❤

On Ann's wedding morning, the owner of the Connecticut restaurant where her reception was to be held called with some bad news: there had been a fire. Already nervous, the bride-to-be started crying and hung up the phone before the owner could explain further.

"It was probably just a kitchen fire," said Ann's father, trying to reassure her. But when no one answered the phone at the restaurant, the bride's mother called the local fire department. The entire restaurant had burned to the ground!

When the ceremony started, the families still didn't know where the reception would be held. At its conclusion, however, the caterer was able to announce that guests were invited to an American Legion Hall in town. Without maps or directions, however, many people got lost—including the reception's disc jockey. While driving by a nearby veteran's lodge, he had noticed a large billboard congratulating Ann, so he pulled in and set up his equipment.

Soon afterward, another disc jockey showed up. Yes, this was the spot for Ann's reception, said the second man—but not the Ann who had hired the first disc jockey. And this was a hall for the Veterans of Foreign Wars—not the American Legion. The first Ann's disc jockey packed up his things and rushed off to the American Legion Hall—two hours late.

Everything worked out in the end—sort of. The owner of the restaurant that went up in smoke served Ann's wedding guests on paper plates, and the guests had to make do without the traditional Italian cookies that were lost in the blaze. "I think they were a little well-done," said Ann.

❤ ❤ ❤

It was an intimate and romantic setting for a wedding. Thirty close friends and family members had gathered at the Colorado home of Paul and Grace. The bride and groom stood with the maid of honor and best man in front of a roaring fire. A row of candles flickered from the mantel.

The officiant was well into his preamble, when the photographer noticed something peculiar through his lens. The bride was aglow—literally! One of the candles had fallen out of its holder and landed near her feet—on her floor-length tulle veil. Silently, he inched over to her side, quietly stomped on the veil to smother the flames, and coolly resumed taking pictures.

❤ ❤ ❤

When Jessica and Bob planned a Christmas wedding reception in the Victorian home of her mother, in New

York, they pictured all the fireplaces merrily burning. When they arrived home after the ceremony, however, they found thick black smoke and shrieking smoke alarms. In the excitement, no one had remembered to open the dampers.

Windows and dampers were quickly opened, and the smoke slowly cleared—but there was a definite chill in the air throughout the festivities.

❤ ❤ ❤

Everyone agreed that the one-hundred-year-old concert hall in New York made a wonderful setting for the reception of Beth and Jim's June wedding.

But just as the disc jockey was formally introducing the bride and groom, his equipment went on the fritz.

"He's pulling too much juice," the house manager was saying, when suddenly the room began to fill up with thick smoke. A transformer in the basement had blown.

The fire was small and no one was hurt. But the thick smoke and the age of the building prompted firemen to evacuate everyone and insist that no one reenter until the wiring could be carefully inspected.

The guests milled about outside, all dressed up with no place to go. "There was not a sequin left in town," recalls the house manager. "They were all here in the street."

Then, one of the guests spotted a teenager passing by with a boom box on his shoulder and offered him ten dollars to stay. They shook on the deal, and within minutes everyone was cutting the rug on the asphalt.

Meanwhile, one of the firemen overheard Beth complaining that the fire had deprived her of the chance to throw her bouquet from the staircase. "No problem," said the accommodating public servant. He lifted the bride up to the cherry picker of the fire truck, and as the video camera whirred, she triumphantly tossed her flowers to the waiting crowd below.

But now the guests were getting hungry. Many of them were out-of-towners, and they were reluctant to call it a day.

American ingenuity to the rescue again. The one hundred and thirty guests walked four blocks to the home of the bride's parents. The manager of the concert hall ordered up buckets of fried chicken from a fast-food place across the street, and bottles of liquor from a nearby bar. The show went on!

In the Drink

It was a beautiful afternoon in early June. The wedding reception was being held in New Jersey, on the fourteenth floor of the groom's oceanfront condo building. Music flowed from the ballroom. The tennis courts, the pool, and the outdoor terraces were all decorated for the occasion. The ceremony went smoothly and the newlyweds and guests sat down for a seven-course gourmet meal.

That was when all hell broke loose.

Two thousand square feet of wet ceiling tile fell on the guests, the food, and the floor. Then, thousands of gallons of water began to pour in from a broken sprinkler line. No one was hurt, but water continued to pour in, flowing down ramps and into the marble lobby. By the end of the flood, there were three to four inches of water on the ballroom floor.

Through it all, the disc jockey kept right on playing. Given the flood-like circumstances, some of the guests wondered why he didn't finish off the reception entertainment with "Sea of Love."

After their guests were shuttled in five yachts to a romantic island off the East Coast, Carol, Harry, and their bridal party began to board their boat, secure in the knowledge that they would arrive in style at the July ceremony.

Ignoring the captain's order to wait so that he could help her board, Carol's grandmother, a large woman, put her foot on the edge of the boat. Her movement pushed the boat away from the dock, leaving her other foot (and the rest of her body) momentarily suspended over the water—before she fell in with a resounding splash.

"She can't swim!" screamed the bride, throwing down her flowers, horror-stricken. The dockmaster threw a line into the water, while three ushers, the best man, and the captain all plunged in to rescue the struggling woman—not an easy task, given her girth. "Flipping her up into the boat took longer than expected," observed one witness wryly.

Grandma was led dripping to the dockmaster's office, where her dry-clean-only silk dress was thrown into a dryer with the ushers' outfits. Two hours later, the still-game matron in the wrinkled dress and the rest of the wedding party belatedly joined guests on the island. The remainder of the day went swimmingly.

❤ ❤ ❤

Celia was determined that her guests would be immersed in a Polynesian atmosphere. The plan was for eight men dressed in South Sea costumes and carrying tiki torches to flank the bride and groom as they entered the country-club ballroom—to oohs, ahs, and thunderous applause, of course.

No one considered that tiki torches generate a lot of heat. No one imagined that the heat would set off the club's sprinkler system.

Everybody in the room got drenched.

❤ ❤ ❤

Wedding ceremonies were frequently held on the patio in front of a twenty-foot reflecting pool at a New Jersey banquet facility. One bride wanted something different; she requested that her vows be exchanged near the columns *behind* the pool.

The owner of the facility advised against this positioning, pointing out that the bride would have to walk all the way around the side of the pool to get to the altar. "Well, then," said the bride matter-of-factly, "I want bridges placed over the pool."

When she heard the cost of having the bridges provided, she insisted on bringing her own. It was a bad idea, said the owner, but as long as she had the proper insurance, he wouldn't stop her.

The day before the ceremony, he watched as the bride's family and friends haphazardly constructed a wooden bridge over the reflecting pool. Because the boards they brought were not quite long enough to span the pool, they nailed them together, then laid more boards crosswise to form a bridge. The owner again took the bride aside and told her he didn't think the present construction would support her weight. "Yes," she re-torted, "but when the pool is filled with water, the wood will float!" It was pointless to argue.

On the wedding day, the groom waited patiently for his bride to approach him via the bridge. The bridge bowed in the center as she crossed, but it miraculously held.

As the ceremony concluded, the bride's family con-gratulated themselves on their engineering acumen. The bride triumphantly took her groom's arm, and together they walked back across the bridge. Quicker than anyone could say "I told you so," the structure completely gave way, and the couple sank in water up to their ankles.

❤ ❤ ❤

Ask any mother who's had her daughter's reception at home and she'll tell you the first thing she did was run out and buy all new plants. But this California bride's family went far beyond that: they had the grounds out back newly landscaped, and, as a wonderfully romantic touch, they built a gazebo by the swimming pool. Under its Victorian domed roof the bride and groom would stand and cut the eight-tier wedding cake.

Shortly before the groom was planning to enter the gazebo, he and some groomsmen started horsing around. Losing his balance meant falling into the pool; to steady himself, the groom grabbed onto the closest thing handy—the gazebo. Down it all came—groom, gazebo, and eight layers of wedding cake—straight into the pool.

A hundred guests stopped sipping their champagne

and held their breaths, stunned. The groom was sopping wet, the cake was forming a buttercream slick on the chlorinated water, the gazebo looked like it had been hit by a hurricane. What could possibly rescue the moment? Luckily, someone had a bright idea—a toast to the bride and groom's happiness!

Some of the groomsmen at Jan and Ron's New York wedding had a little too much of the party spirit. They stripped down to their underwear and began diving into the New York country club's pool. Unamused, the banquet manager appeared and told the ushers to get out of the water and get their clothes back on. All but one managed to make a relatively graceful exit. The last aquanaut lost his shorts climbing out of the water and had to streak across the lawn.

At an outdoor wedding in California, the overzealous photographer kept directing Bonnie to step back so he could get all of her magnificent dress in a full-length outdoor shot. All of a sudden, the bride felt a slight tug on her dress, and turned to find that her train had dipped into the swimming pool behind her. She leaned over to extricate it, but the material was so voluminous and heavy that it dragged her right into the water.

The hairdresser was able to patch up Bonnie's hair and makeup relatively fast, but the bridesmaid who attempted to blow-dry her clothes had less luck. The satin was shriveled; the illusion veil looked like a limp shower curtain. Dampened but not daunted, the bride changed into her perfectly pressed going-away dress, and the party continued.

❤ ❤ ❤

The only trouble with having a really great reception is that no one wants it to end. Laura and Peter's California reception was a classic good time—made even more so by a gag gift they received for their Hawaii honeymoon: two pairs of oversized fluorescent-colored surfer shorts. Peter donned his shorts over his tuxedo, making him look like a formally dressed beach bum on the dance floor.

As the evening wore on, the couple exchanged nervous looks. They had a plane to catch, but how could they leave the reception in full swing? They decided to put a damper on things—nicely, of course.

Still wearing her headpiece, the bride changed into her bathing suit (packed in her bag for the Hawaii vacation) and her giant shorts. Now matching her groom, shorts-wise, she grabbed his hand and together they ran across the street to the ocean and jumped in.

But the newly married couple underestimated their friends' party spirit. The bridesmaids and groomsmen stripped down to various stages of undress—from boxer shorts and slips to nothing at all—and followed Laura and Peter into the surf!

We're Not in Kansas Anymore

At two a.m. on the morning of his August wedding, William was awakened by a phone call from a local civic leader. Hurricane Elena was scheduled to hit his Florida community that day, he said, and evacuees would have to be sheltered at the church where William and his fiancée, Roseanne, were to be married.

When the ceremony began at three-thirty p.m., only twelve invited guests had been able to make it to the church. Evacuees—in bathrobes and curlers—filled the empty pews. Roseanne and William's wedding-night hotel had been evacuated as well, so the couple spent their first night of wedded bliss watching TV weather reports with their in-laws.

♥ ♥ ♥

Ross and Monica's wedding was the day after Hurricane Gloria hit the New York area in September 1985. Maureen's house had no electricity or telephone. "I had no idea how I was going to put on my makeup or do my hair," she recalls. "But people helped us out. One neighbor brought a generator so I could blow-dry my hair. Others drove up and down the highway trying to convince several businesses to close early so we could borrow a generator, which would have made it possible for the band to play at our reception site." Since there was no electricity or music in the church, the couple lit candles. A folksinger, who was to sing during the ceremony, also performed the processional.

As if Mother Nature hadn't had enough sport with the couple, a swarm of bees from a fallen tree attacked the bridal party as they stood outside for a group portrait. The group quickly scattered and continued the photograph session inside.

The bad weather seemed to rattle everyone. First, the maître d' forgot the couple's names as he introduced them to the guests. Then, when interviewed for the wedding video, the bride's own grandfather had to ask his wife for the couple's names before he wished them luck.

The honeymoon to Saint John and Saint Thomas should have been a nice respite—and it was for two days. The rest of the time, they were in the middle of Tropical Storm Isabella. And, in a crowning touch of unlikely bad luck, just two days after they returned, Long Island experienced an earthquake!

❤ ❤ ❤

Meg and Hal had hoped for a rustic, old-fashioned wedding—but they didn't think that would require them to relive the Great Trek Westward.

On the day of their wedding, however, the heaviest flooding the Napa Valley had ever seen made travel conditions not unlike those faced by the pioneers. Mud was everywhere, and fallen trees had knocked out power lines and blocked roads. But when Meg's father and her groom encountered one such obstacle, they refused to be daunted. They returned home for a chainsaw, drove back to the tree, sawed their way through, and arrived at the church just forty minutes late.

The wedding guests were of similar hardy stock—and those who needed help got it from the cavalry—in this case, the California State Highway Patrol, who were out on the roads in full force during the emergency.

In a lovely and absolutely unplanned touch, the wedding was plunged back into the twentieth century at just the right moment. As the best man lifted his glass of sparkling Chandon to toast the couple's happiness, the lights came back on!

❤ ❤ ❤

The earth moves for many couples, but Lisa and Andy didn't anticipate that a real earthquake would hit the San Francisco Bay area eleven days before their October wedding.

As a result of the quake, their wedding site was condemned, but the couple were able to book a hotel ballroom at the eleventh hour. Then Lisa heard that her dry-cleaner's building had collapsed as well—trapping her wedding gown inside. She finally reached the owner at his home (phone lines were down throughout the city), and was greeted with the good news: he had removed her dress from the building before it had been condemned, too.

Dark cloud number three descended on the wedding day. Under normal circumstances, the florist had an hour's drive to the wedding site. But with the Bay Bridge closed because of the earthquake, he arrived at the church more than two hours late—after the guests were already seated.

Everyone watched sympathetically as the harried florist tried to work at breakneck speed. Then came the silver lining: the guests got up from their seats and volunteered to lend a hand hanging garlands and positioning altar arrangements.

The result may not have been exactly what the florist envisioned, but the enormous goodwill more than made up for any misplanted blossoms—and the ceremony started almost on time.

❤ ❤ ❤

One Fourth of July, lightning knocked out the power at a banquet hall in New Jersey, just as a young couple exchanged their first newlywed kiss. The guests believed it had been staged for dramatic effect—until they saw the firemen, who had been alerted by an automatic alarm. No one seemed to mind, though, and the reception continued with an unamplified band and dancing by candlelight.

Later, along with a thank-you card, the bride and groom sent the banquet manager a wedding photograph:

the two of them formally dressed, wearing fire helmets and sitting on a fire engine.

♥ ♥ ♥

Leo and Marcella thought surviving an explosion outside their New York City apartment that had killed three people was traumatic enough. But three days later, they learned that when the huge steam pipe burst, asbestos had been spewed over the area, and immediate evacuation of the building was necessary. They would be put up in a hotel, but all their possessions were off-limits—including Marcella's wedding shoes and veil, Leo's heirloom wedding ring, the honeymoon clothes, passports and plane tickets, and the guest list.

Fortunately, the couple were given enough money to replace the wedding accessories—and a week before the wedding, a worker who was a sucker for romance took pity on Leo and retrieved the abandoned ring.

♥ WEDDING FROM HELL NO. 6 ♥

Bruce's bad luck started a week before his September wedding in North Carolina. First he learned that the Virgin Islands, his honeymoon destination, had been devastated by Hurricane Hugo. Then the plane he had boarded in New York City bound for North Carolina and his bride, Margie, skidded off the runway at LaGuardia Airport and into the water. Bruce was fished out by a rescue boat, but his luggage, with all of his wedding clothes, ended up at the bottom of the East River.

The next day, he and some friends decided to drive to the wedding site. Three hours away, Bruce called Margie, who told him that Hugo was headed directly for their town! Hotels there, including the rehearsal-dinner and reception sites, had all been evacuated.

The groom and his friends stayed overnight at a hotel in a nearby town. The next morning, they learned that the storm had bypassed the wedding site, and the rest of their drive was uneventful. The bad-luck streak was broken, the wedding went according to plan, and only the honeymoon had to be postponed until hurricane season had blown over.

CHAPTER 7

Wedding Services from The Twilight Zone

❤ ❤ ❤

A wedding consultant can speak up for your interests and work with professionals to achieve what you might not have been able to do otherwise.

—From *BRIDE'S* magazine

❤ ❤ ❤

Let Them Eat Cake

Sometime in the past, the mother of the Michigan bride had tasted an absolutely delicious cake—so dense and rich that its flavor still lingered in her memory. Determined that her daughter's wedding should be unforgettable in every way, she began her quest to re-create the dessert in the form of the ultimate wedding cake.

Having found the recipe, she commissioned an expert pastry chef to execute it with flair. The chef advised against stacking such a dense cake in layers, but the bride's mother insisted on all five tiers. The cake was duly baked, stacked, and elaborately decorated.

The next day, on her way from the ceremony to the reception, the bride walked through the dining area to take one last look at her gorgeous five-tier cake on display. As it turned out, it *was* a last look. The guests never got to see it at all.

A half-hour before the reception began, the wedding consultant was grabbed by the caterer and dragged into the kitchen. The only people who were going to get a taste of the cake were the kitchen help—who were licking their fingers as they attempted to salvage something from what now appeared to be a rich chocolate hash. The cake was so dense that it had collapsed under its own weight.

❤ ❤ ❤

The Michigan reception was nearly over and the guests began to make their departures. Standing near the hallway door, the wedding consultant overheard one annoyed woman exclaim to her companion, "Did you notice? There isn't any cake to take home!"

The consultant ran into the ballroom to check. Sure enough, the caterer had neglected to cut the cake and box it in take-away "good-luck" tradition for the guests. In fact, it later turned out that the caterer was in a feud with the pastry chef, who had been hired independently by the bride. After the cake-cutting photographs had been taken, the caterer had wheeled the cake behind a pillar and left it there to remain hidden for the rest of the party.

❤ ❤ ❤

The maître d' at the New York catering hall prided himself on the elegant manner in which he balanced a serving tray on just three fingers. But three fingers proved not to be enough when he tripped at a wedding while holding the wedding cake. The cake went flying and smashed against the wall—where it stuck quite impressively.

❤ ❤ ❤

At precisely the proper moment at the reception, the dining-room hostess at the country-club wedding in Connecticut gathered Becky, her groom, Barry, and their 175 guests over to one corner table. There, the beautifully decorated wedding cake with whipped-cream frosting had been placed on a custom-designed white eyelet-and-ribbon tablecloth.

The floorboards of the room were uneven, however, and the top layer of the cake began to slide noticeably backward. The photographer was already positioned to take the all-important shot of the bride and groom cutting their cake, and it was too late to interrupt.

The wedding consultant decided it was her job to save the day. She wedged herself in back of the cake table, crouched down on the floor, and raised the tablecloth over her head. Thus hidden, she was able to hold the top layer of the cake upright. The photographer snapped away.

When Becky and Barry were looking over their wedding proofs, they burst out laughing when they came to the cake-cutting shots. The processed film revealed a smiling bride and groom—and two legs in high heels protruding from the back of the table.

❤ ❤ ❤

The California country club chosen by Kevin and Kathy was not known for its food, so the couple decided to order the wedding cake from an outside vendor—and spare no expense. "We thought we'd send people home with a memory of a magnificent and delicious dessert," recalls Kevin.

After tasting many pastry chefs' creations, they finally decided on an incredibly expensive three-tier whipped-cream-and-chocolate extravaganza known as Chocolate Decadence. They decided they might as well splurge on the cake topper, too—a Lladro porcelain figurine of a bride and groom.

Since the whipped-cream topping was four inches thick and melted easily, delivery time was crucial. The wedding was on a Sunday, so the pastry chef decided to make and freeze the cake in advance. He would then deliver it five hours ahead of time so that it would be defrosted in plenty of time to be eaten after the dinner.

When the bridal couple walked in, the cake was on display, looking magnificent—except for one thing. In the hours that the cake had been sitting, the ten-inch Lladro figurine had decided to go skiing! It had slid off the top of the cake and schussed a path through the whipped cream, all the way down to the bottom tier.

The wedding consultant swiftly put the figurine back on top and smoothed out the whipped cream, but the porcelain couple decided it was time to take another run, and skied down again.

The wedding consultant was determined that Kevin and Kathy would have photographs of the cake-cutting with the cake exactly as the couple had planned it—with the porcelain figurine on top. Once again, she placed the delicate bride and groom atop the cake.

When it began to teeter yet again, the flesh-and-blood

bride and groom gave up. Besides, they wanted to save the figurine as a memento of their wedding, and were starting to fear that it would wipe out on the slopes and crash to the floor.

Kevin removed the topper and placed it on a side table. Then he and Kathy positioned themselves to cut the cake, their hands wrapped in the traditional manner around the knife handle. The blade easily glided through the four-inch layer of whipped cream, then stopped abruptly. The cake's Decadent Chocolate interior was still frozen rock-solid.

The couple attempted to saw a piece out of the frozen

WEDDING PORTRAIT
Luci Baines Johnson Weds Patrick Nugent

❤ ❤ ❤

First attempts to cut the seven-layer, fourteen-tier, three-hundred-pound summer fruitcake proved futile at the White House reception of Luci Baines Johnson and Patrick Nugent on August 6, 1966. President Johnson stepped in and after repeated efforts, using the sword knife given as a wedding gift to the couple by Senator and Mrs. Birch Bayh of Indiana, the *trio* finally broke through the icing.

mass, and eventually managed to put a few crumbs and a lot of whipped cream on a plate—which they then pretended to feed each other for the pictures.

❤ ❤ ❤

The morning of Tina's Minnesota wedding, the care-taker came in to unlock the reception hall, leaving his German-shepherd police dog free to wander. The cater-ers came in and began setting up, the cake was delivered, and the forgotten dog continued to wander aimlessly about the grounds. Two hours before the reception was to start, the dog discovered an open door, entered the hall, and took a big bite out of the wedding cake.

The caterer shooed the dog away in time to save the bulk of the cake. He cut away the eaten part, filled it in with icing, and turned the repaired area toward the wall. The bride and groom never knew.

❤ ❤ ❤

As a tribute to her parents' European heritage, Nicole ordered something very special for her California wed-ding reception. It was a traditional French *croquem-bouche*—a confectionary stack of caramelized puff pastries, precariously held together with elaborate sugar bows.

As the hour for the celebration approached, however, the bride noticed that there was no *croquembouche* in sight. Since it measured five feet from top to bottom, she knew it wasn't something easily misplaced. A quick call to the bakery confirmed her worst fears: despite the fact that the establishment was just around the block, the deliveryman had been driving around for two hours, looking for the reception site.

The delicate dessert did survive the trek up and down the San Francisco hills, and even arrived on time. The bakery's owner arrived too—apologizing profusely and berating his staff in three different languages.

❤ ❤ ❤

Deborah's plan was to cut—not catch—the cake at her November New York wedding. But just as she and her husband, Tom, were about to do the honors with their five-layer white wedding cake with burgundy roses, the video man tripped over some wires and banged against the round dessert table, causing the top two layers to lurch off the cake.

Having not a thought for their formal wear, the bride and groom rushed toward the confection avalanche—arms outstretched—and caught the mass of buttercream and sponge cake in their bare hands.

The bride wondered if it would be anticlimactic to throw her bouquet as well.

❤ ❤ ❤

Sally kept her cool throughout her wedding dinner—even though the caterer failed to give the guests the agreed-upon fruit-salad appetizer, even though *all* the entrées were Florentine style, instead of there being a choice of almondine and Florentine dishes. No, this was one bride determined not to blow up. She calmly let the caterer know about the error and proceeded to enjoy her reception.

But when the wedding cake was wheeled out, Sally

WEDDING PORTRAIT
Roseanne Barr Weds Tom Arnold

♥ ♥ ♥

When actress Roseanne Barr married her second husband, Tom Arnold, in February 1990, at her Benedict Canyon, California, home, the traditional custom of the bride and groom feeding each other a piece of cake got out of hand.

The cake went beyond elaborate. The first layer was chocolate with Bavarian-cream filling, and was covered with white-chocolate icing. The second and third layers were of carrot cake with cream cheese and apricot frosting. White orchids of different sizes decorated each tier, and elaborate latticework covered the sides.

By the time the customary cake-cutting was over, both bride and groom had eaten two entire tiers of the cake themselves; their faces, hair, and clothes were covered with icing and crumbs. Needless to say, this less than appetizing spectacle ensured that plenty of cake was left over for the first anniversary.

was pushed too far. She had specifically requested that the cake be topped with fresh flowers instead of the often-used plastic bride-and-groom cake topper. And there was her cake—complete with plastic figures crowning the top layer!

Hell hath no fury like a bride betrayed. Sally stormed into the kitchen and insisted the caterer remove the cake and fix it *now*—or else.

Several minutes later, it reemerged, with fresh flowers on top, and the cake-cutting began.

❤ ❤ ❤

The lights dimmed. A hush came over the seated guests. The band struck up a Strauss waltz. The stage was set for the presentation of an elaborate Viennese pastry table at the wedding of Michelle and Sean in a posh hotel in New York.

A spotlight focused on a small area of the dance floor as a waiter wheeled out a table stacked high with fine china, crystal, champagne, and assorted fancy cakes and other sweets. Suddenly, the rolling Viennese table collapsed, hurling all of the contents to the ground. All that was left of the once elegant pastries: a mass of whipped cream and the smell of cinnamon.

Luckily, the wedding cake was on display elsewhere in the room.

❤ ❤ ❤

A quick stop at the mall en route to a wedding reception nearly ended in disaster for the baker who was delivering the wedding cake for two Los Angeles–area entertainers. Not until he arrived at the reception site did he realize that the bottom tier of the three-layer cake had been stolen from his car while it was parked at the mall.

The bakery staff quickly made up another tier and returned with it to the hall—only to discover that the frosting style and texture of the other two layers were entirely different; the new layer was no match for the other two, which were decorated with basket weaves, flowers, and poufs. The quick-thinking wedding consultant covered up the mismatch with an array of fresh flowers around the cake's base just as cake-cutting time approached. "Thank goodness cutting the cake is one of the last things the couple does!" the consultant said.

❤ ❤ ❤

Three hundred people showed up in black tie to celebrate the London wedding of an heiress and a barrister. As the ceremony was beginning, the meticulous wedding consultant inspected the cake and found it not to his liking. He immediately called in a second pastry chef and had the entire cake redecorated.

When it was time to present the magnificent five-tier cake to the guests, the icing was still soft from having been reworked. Then, as the cake was being carried out to the reception, the top tier slid off and fell to the ground, destroyed.

The wedding consultant grabbed a floral centerpiece from one of the tables and affixed it to where the top tier once sat. Crossing his fingers, he had the cake wheeled out. Perhaps no one would get close enough to notice, he hoped.

He was right. As they peered at the cake from across the enormous banquet room, everyone remarked that the

---

WEDDING PORTRAIT
Tricia Nixon Weds Edward Cox

♥ ♥ ♥

White House bakers were sorry that they ever thought of circulating a scaled-down version (ten egg whites for a twelve-inch cake) of Tricia Nixon's lemon sponge wedding cake before her White House wedding on June 12, 1971. The idea was that every home throughout the nation could savor the same cake as the White House bride on her wedding day.

But something was terribly wrong with the scaled-down recipe. Eruptions of lemon lava gummed up cookers from coast to coast. There were tales of it hitting the ceiling and flowing over floors! It was like soap on the outside and glue on the inside. Although the original 350-pound cantilevered cake was a great success, a red-faced White House chef had to distribute a revised recipe.

smashing spun-sugar flowers on top were *incredibly* life-like—and wasn't it awfully clever how they matched the floral arrangements on the table?

♥ ♥ ♥

It was time to cut the cake at the New Jersey reception. The bride delicately fed her groom a bite of the first slice. Then the groom pushed the entire top layer in his new wife's face.

The bride, who wore contact lenses, got cake in her eye and ran off to the bathroom for the better part of an hour. Her brother ran over to the table, grabbed the second layer, and threw it full force at the groom. Guests scrambled to get out of the way as the pair further dispensed with cake and started swinging their fists.

It later turned out that the groom's boss had dared him to layer the bride. In fact, he had offered the young man a thousand dollars if he went through with the bombardment.

♥ ♥ ♥

Celeste knew she was marrying a practical joker. But she never suspected that on her wedding day, the joke would literally be on her.

When the two were called up before one hundred guests to cut their wedding cake, Rick was not content to merely feed Celeste a slice. Instead, he removed the entire top tier—which is traditionally saved to be eaten on the couple's first anniversary—and threw it full-force in her face.

The bride, in shock, retreated to the kitchen to clean up—and lost a contact lens in the process. Luckily for Rick, however, his new wife had a sense of humor. (With only one contact lens, she couldn't effectively retaliate, anyway.)

❤ ❤ ❤

It would have taken a pretty dense guest not to guess the theme of Mindy's reception. Reception favors were miniature bears wearing pink ribbon collars imprinted with the names of the bride and groom. There were teddy bears in the floral centerpieces, bears imprinted on the cocktail napkins, and two large, adorable bears dressed up as a bride and groom standing proudly by the head table.

The *teddy de resistance*, however, was on top of a luscious Saint Honore cream wedding cake: a hand-blown ornament of a glass heart containing two glass bears. To showcase it, the caterer had placed the cake in front of a glass wall looking out on a garden.

It was the kind of day every bride hopes for—a beautiful summer day, warm and sunny. So warm and sunny, in fact, that when Mindy walked into the reception site just prior to the guests' arrival, she saw that her beautiful cake was melting—and her hand-blown bear ornament had slid off the top and lay broken on the floor.

Mindy burst into tears. The caterer rung her hands, and the banquet manager had no solution. The photographer, however, took one look at the scene and knew what was called for: epoxy glue. He stuck the fallen pieces of glass heart and bears back together as best he could, and made it look good enough to grace the top of the repaired cake—now safely repositioned in the shade.

❤ ❤ ❤

Just before the country-club wedding in California, the caterer, florist, and disc jockey were attending to last-minute details. The bride's domineering mother came running in, and proceeded to peer over shoulders and nitpick: that tablecloth was too long, the speakers were not facing enough toward the dance floor, the floral centerpieces were not exactly centered.

She then turned her critical eye on the four-tier wedding cake. One of the columns in the top tier was ever-so-slightly crooked—this was completely unacceptable. She reached up to adjust it, knocking the top tier off completely, and decapitating the custom-made candy bride-and-groom cake topper.

For once, she was at a loss. The caterer grimly but efficiently replaced the tier and turned the damaged side to the wall. A hardier if somewhat tackier plastic bride and groom was found to replace the forlornly headless figures, who were consigned to the trash.

Floral Fiascos

Margaret, a Connecticut wedding consultant, was coordinating the August nuptials of her daughter, Vicky, and her daughter's fiancé, Brian. The couple were to be married at an outdoor ceremony at a nearby country inn—in the middle of a record-breaking heat wave.

On Thursday morning, two days before the wedding, Margaret drove in her air-conditioned car to Hartford to pick up their order of special flowers—white bridal roses and soft mauve Margaux lilies—which would be arranged in white lace bridal baskets and placed around the altar. Once back in her unair-conditioned home, she placed the blooms in buckets and buckets of ice water spread throughout the house. At best, she knew, it was a stopgap measure. They'll never make it to the wedding, she thought to herself.

A seasoned veteran of the bridal business, Margaret knew that desperate times required desperate measures. She booked an air-conditioned room in a hotel and checked in with the buckets of flowers as her luggage. After two tedious days of tending the flowers and changing their water around the clock, an exhausted mother of the bride drove her precious cargo to the wedding site. The heat may have been wilting, but every flower stayed as fresh as the day they were picked.

❤ ❤ ❤

Twenty-five years earlier, Fern and Elliot had been married in city hall. Now they planned to make up for all the pomp they had missed, with a black-tie ceremony and celebration for two hundred outside Washington, D.C.

Two florists were hired: one to do the church floral arrangements, the other to create the bouquets. In keeping with the red-and-white color scheme, designed to complement the church's interior, the bridesmaids would carry red gladioli and white spider mums tied with red ribbons. The bride would carry a dozen red roses.

When the bridal consultant opened the flower boxes at the church, she was horrified to see gladioli in the maids' bouquets that were far from red—in fact, they were pumpkin-colored, and clashed horribly with the roses and the church.

It was already after five p.m. and the florist shop was closed. The consultant got additional stems of white mums and gladioli from another shop, pulled apart the bouquets, removed the pumpkin flowers, added the new white blossoms, and retied the bouquets with the red ribbons.

She also suggested that flowers be omitted from pre-wedding photos. While the photographer arranged the wedding party, the consultant rearranged the blooms.

❤ ❤ ❤

When Denise planned her Labor Day wedding to Jeff, she was determined that the flowers be extra special. The wedding was to be in a synagogue in New York, and she hired a florist who was an hour away, because of his fine reputation.

The wedding was scheduled for one p.m. The florist had assured Denise that he would arrive by nine-thirty a.m. to start decorating. But by ten-thirty, he had yet to arrive. Then the caterer told her that the florist had just left a message. The truck had run into problems, but not to worry—he was sending a backup.

When a few more hours had gone by and the wedding countdown had begun, the bride's mother ran out to a local florist and bought a rose for the bride and a carnation for her groom, recalls Denise. The caterer pitched in by bringing in silk trees from his office. The wedding went on, bare of any other greenery and blossoms.

A few days after the wedding, Denise contacted the florist. "He said the truck somehow had mistakenly gotten on a parkway ramp where commercial vehicles aren't allowed and had been impounded by the police." And the flowers? "He told me as the police were lifting the truck to drag it away, all the flowers fell out and people looted them."

"It was a pretty shaky story," notes Denise. "I know for a fact that they don't impound trucks for driving on the wrong parkway. His 'fine reputation' has wilted."

❤ ❤ ❤

"Flowers are very important to me, and I wanted them to be an important part of my wedding," says Karen, a Kentucky bride. "Specifically, I wanted the color scheme built around a red rose, and I told the florist that the first day. She wrote it down and I didn't think too much about it.

"I went about my business coordinating the dresses around the color red," she continues. "When the wedding got closer, I called her a couple of times to confirm, and everything was okay."

But things were not okay, as Karen discovered when she arrived at the church for her November wedding. "The flowers were supposed to be there at four-thirty p.m. They weren't; they got there at seven p.m.—too late to do preceremony pictures. Worst of all, there wasn't one red rose in the bunch! I had white roses, my bridesmaids had fuchsia carnations, and both of the mothers' bouquets were dead!"

After the honeymoon, Karen's husband went to talk to the florist, who denied Karen had ordered red roses, and said that she hadn't paid enough for roses, in any case. "She read him the riot act and told him I didn't know what I wanted," says Karen. "At that point, we decided to sue."

In small-claims court, the couple were awarded the 340-dollar florist's fee. The florist appealed the decision—and also filed for bankruptcy, which means she may not have to pay any of her disgruntled customers.

❤ ❤ ❤

An hour before the California bridal party was to leave for the church, the bride's cousin arrived. Although the cousin's health had been deteriorating, she still had insisted on doing the flowers. When the four bridesmaids went to lift their flowers from the boxes, they realized that they were one bouquet short. Unless someone did some quick thinking, one bridesmaid would have to go empty-handed.

No one wanted to tell the cousin and risk hurting her feelings—there was nothing she could do at that point anyway. And the bride was by then an emotional disaster. No, it was up to the resourceful bridesmaids to save the day.

So the attendants sent a friend to the nearest florist for a bouquet holder and some ferns to serve as a filler for all of the bouquets. They then disassembled the three bouquets and gave themselves a crash course in flower arranging.

Twenty minutes later, the bridal party left for the church with time to spare, a grateful bride and four pretty—if now somewhat petite—bouquets in tow.

❤ ❤ ❤

Joan and Tommy wanted a wedding full of flowers— lots and lots of flowers. They had the aisle lined with troughs of flowers, each supported by two wooden poles. Trailing vines and floral garlands cascaded eight feet from the containers to the ground, creating the illusion of a floral wall on either side of the aisle.

Naturally, Joan wanted her reception to be florally festive as well. So when the room in the New York City hotel was being rearranged for the party, she asked that the troughs be moved near the dining tables, so the guests would feel as if they were eating in a bower of flowers.

It was every bit as impressive as she hoped. But halfway through dinner, a creaking was heard, followed by the ominous sound of cracking wood. Joan and Tommy looked up just in time to see one of the supporting stakes holding a floral trough give way and fall toward a table of dining reception guests.

Luckily, the crashing shrubbery just missed the table and crashed onto the floor. No one was hurt, and the remaining floral displays were moved to outside corners of the room, out of harm's way.

❤ ❤ ❤

Jessica and Matthew planned to marry aboard a ship and set sail with guests for a California coast harbor-cruise reception. The guests assembled at the pier on schedule, but the florist had been given the wrong directions by the couple and missed the boat—arriving a good hour after the floating party had already gotten underway.

The seaworthy couple didn't make waves; they merely said their vows without bouquets and boutonnieres. As

for the florist, her frenzied waving caught the ship captain's attention, and he set a course straight for her and
the flower arrangements. Permission to board was
granted.

Musical Mishaps

A church in Ohio employed a lovely elderly woman to play the organ for all functions. She was known to have occasional moments of befuddlement, but she always soldiered on as if nothing had happened.

One such moment of disorientation occurred in the midst of a wedding, as the bride began to walk down the aisle. There was a brief silence, and then music began anew: a rousing rendition of "You're a Grand Old Flag"!

❤ ❤ ❤

The wedding reception was going to be at the Empire Room, the California bandleader told his group. The piano player didn't bother to write down the address—he had just played at the Empire Room and knew where to go. Little did he realize he was entering The Twilight Zone. . . .

The day of the wedding, the piano player arrived on time at the Empire Room. No band, no bride, nobody. He proceeded up the street to another major hotel that also had an Empire Room. Empty.

He tried telephoning the bandleader, but he had evidently left for the right Empire Room and the answering service didn't know anything about it. Frantic, the piano player went to another major hotel, ran to the Empire Room and found . . . nothing.

Two hours and seven major hotels later, he hit the right one.

❤ ❤ ❤

Beverly thought she heard buzzing as she was walking down the aisle at her August wedding in New York. Since she was so nervous and distracted that she could barely see the altar, though, she thought it was just a symptom of stress.

Later, she found out that the hall had not had time to move the baby grand piano from another floor prior to her ceremony. Before the bride made her entrance, the rabbi told the guests that they would have to provide the music. The buzzing Beverly heard was 150 guests humming "Here Comes the Bride" as she made her way to the altar.

"I was too nervous to notice where the buzzing was coming from," Beverly now says, laughing. "Afterward, people came up to me and said, 'What a wonderful idea to have group participation!' "

❤ ❤ ❤

As the band members were setting up their equipment before a wedding in New York, one of the guests approached the bandleader, pointed out another guest, and said, "See that man over there? Don't let him sing with you!" The bandleader shrugged. He had seen it all; whenever a lot of relatives were assembled, this sort of thing was bound to happen.

He didn't even think twice when a second guest came up with the same request, pointing out the same man. "Whatever you do," the second guest begged, "don't let that man sit in." Even a third warning from yet another guest did not faze him. But by the time a sixth and seventh person had said, "We *don't* want to hear him sing," the bandleader began to take them seriously. Preventing this guy from a solo performance was obviously going to be tough.

And indeed it was. Throughout the evening, the would-be singer kept coming up to the band, and the musician kept ignoring him. Finally, in the middle of a song, the unwanted guest just walked up, wrested the microphone out of the singer's hand, and as relatives cringed, began to sing.

The band used a tactic that always works with atonal hams as well as kindergartners: he signaled his band to stop playing until the unruly relative handed back the mike.

❤ ❤ ❤

The church had been having problems with the organ and had called the repairman, but he failed to arrive in time for the Saturday morning wedding. When the organist began to play, she was relieved to hear that the instrument had temporarily recovered and was emanating music at full sound as the bridesmaids and ushers processed.

Then, when the bride was halfway down the aisle, the organ gave out completely—the only sound now was the whoosh of the pedals. The bride completed her walk to the altar stony faced, in utter silence.

❤ ❤ ❤

When the band arrived at the wedding site in New York, they were pleased to see that a platform had been built for them under a tent in the backyard. The afternoon was quite warm; it would be nice to play in the shade.

As they were setting up, however, they noticed that the piano kept rolling downhill—the tent people had neglected to make the platform completely level. Attempts were made to nail the piano to the platform, and somehow the band played on without mishap in spite of the piano listing throughout the sets.

❤ ❤ ❤

Emily, a Virginia bride, was sixty-one and finally marrying her childhood sweetheart. Although she had been married before, she had never had a church wedding—and she was determined that it should be as majestic and splendid as anything England's Royal Family could muster.

As for her processional, she told the organist that she definitely did not want the "Wedding March." It simply wasn't majestic enough—especially for a bride of her maturity. The organist searched her repertoire and came up with what she was sure would be a splendid alternative.

On the appointed day, nearly eight hundred guests gathered at the church. The ushers, bridesmaids, maid of honor, ring bearer, and flower girl had all gone down the aisle and it was time for the bride to make her grand entrance. The organist began the first few bars of "Trumpet Voluntary," infusing each chord with as much majesty as she could. Emily did not appear.

The organist was a little uneasy, but assumed Emily had encountered a minor last-minute hitch. More minutes passed, however, and the organist reached the last page of music. Where was the bride?

Just then, the wedding director crawled over from behind the floral arrangements and hissed at the organist, "Psssst. Emily says she won't walk down the aisle unless you play 'Here Comes the Bride.' "

"She insisted that she didn't want that piece played," the organist cried. "I didn't even bring the music!"

But the bride wouldn't budge.

It was an organist's worst nightmare—being at a wedding and leaving the music at home—and it was coming true. Well, the organist thought, I've played "Here Comes the Bride" enough times. Maybe if I play slowly and Emily walks quickly, I'll be able to remember enough of it to get her down the aisle.

She began the piece, then looked up. Emily was walking slower than any bride ever had. This was her crowning moment and she wanted to prolong it as long as possible.

Then the wedding director reappeared from behind the bank of flowers. "Pssst,"—she motioned excitedly— "I found this piano music in the music library!"

Relieved, the organist took the music, then noticed that it was written in the key of F. She had already begun playing in the key of C.

Wagner may have rolled over in his grave to hear the transition the frazzled organist improvised, but the key switch was made and the bride got down the aisle.

❤ ❤ ❤

The bride told the harpist and violinist weeks before the wedding that she wanted a specific aria to be played for her walk down the aisle. But as she began her majestic steps, she heard not the familiar melody she expected, but a monotonous series of chords. The musicians were playing the wrong section of the musical piece—not the aria at all, but the *recitative*, which is just incidental music under the dialogue, entirely without a beat. Unsuccessful in finding any rhythm she could step to, the bride stumbled to the altar as quickly as possible.

❤ ❤ ❤

The New Jersey wedding ceremony was nearly over, but it looked like the band for the reception was never going to show up. The banquet manager hurriedly thumbed through his Rolodex and called every musician he knew, leaving the same message on every machine: if you're free to play this evening, come over—pronto.

In the end, he assembled a fairly decent ensemble, considering the eight or nine musicians had never before played together. And when they took a break, the *two* disc jockeys took over!

Photographic Follies

Sarah and Richard hired a four-man video crew to capture every second of their wedding. The audio man was hooked up to a wireless mike, which picked up every word and sound.

Upon returning from their honeymoon, the bride and groom sat down to view the final tape. As they watched themselves cut the cake, they noticed an odd sound of trickling water in the background. "Was there a fountain in the room?" Sarah asked Richard.

Then they heard the unmistakable sound of a flush. The audio man had forgotten to turn himself off before going to the men's room.

❤ ❤ ❤

Douglas and Susan loved the mountains, so on their January wedding day, they were driven in a horse-drawn carriage two hundred feet up a mountain pass in Colorado. There, they joined the officiant, guests, and photographer on the plateau of an experts' ski slope.

As the ceremony began, the photographer was hard at work, taking pictures from every angle. Then, to get more of the inspiring vista behind the couple into the picture, he backed up several steps—and dropped from sight!

Appalled, the wedding party ran to the mountain's edge and looked down. There, they saw a human snow-man—limbs and camera sticking out—rolling down the slope. There was a ghastly silence as he hit bottom. Then everyone burst into relieved applause as the photographer stood up and showed himself to be unharmed. The wedding resumed.

Just as the rings were being exchanged, a snowmobile arrived at the ceremony site. Out jumped the irrepressible photographer, clicking away.

❤ ❤ ❤

The father of the bride had carefully tucked the cash to pay for the reception in his tuxedo jacket pocket. When the band started playing the horah and the room heated up, he removed his jacket, hung it on the back of his chair, and continued dancing. There was nothing to worry about—everyone present was a relative or a dear friend.

Later that afternoon, the caterer asked for payment and the father reached into his pocket—the envelope was gone. Embarrassed, the father quickly asked relatives to contribute cash from their own wallets, so that the bill could be paid in full.

The mystery of the missing cash remained unsolved. Weeks later, the bride's family gathered to watch the newly arrived videotape of the wedding day. The camera panned this way and that, capturing all the merriment for posterity. It also captured the groom's father pocketing the cash.

The next week, the groom's family was invited for dinner—and a special screening of the video. Needless to say, the cash was repaid in full.

♥ ♥ ♥

Robert and Susan assumed that their photographer would simply *know* that they wanted a photo of each table of guests at their reception in Illinois, so they would have a record of everyone who attended. When their proofs came back, however, they were missing shots of key family members and guests. Their photographer explained that he had taken pictures of people he "liked"—not Aunt Minnie or Grandpa Joe, but "those with interesting faces."

♥ ♥ ♥

Maureen knew she wanted the photos of her New Jersey wedding to have a soft-focus look. When she saw an ad for a New York City–based photography company specializing in romantically styled pictures, she thought the company would be perfect.

A year before her May wedding, Maureen and her fiancé, Ray, met with a salesperson. They were introduced to two pleasant women, described as the photographer and her assistant. Maureen paid a required $500 deposit that day and sent in another $500 three months before the wedding. (The last $500 was to be paid afterward.)

On her wedding day, however, a male photographer and a male assistant arrived. "The photographer was filthy dirty," recalls Maureen. "He smelled. His shirt was open halfway down his chest. His hair wasn't combed. He was rude to guests."

Afterward, the company told Maureen that she would be charged $75 dollars if she didn't show up for her proof selection appointment. Worse, the company was open only a few days a week, from midmorning to midafternoon. Maureen, who worked from nine a.m. to five p.m. in another state, couldn't go without taking a day off.

When she selected proofs in August, Maureen was dismayed. The photos were definitely not soft-focus. And when she asked whether her pictures would be ready to send as Christmas gifts, the owner replied, "It takes six months." Finally, he agreed to send a few single photos. They never arrived.

The albums that were to be ready that February never materialized. Maureen's weekly calls to the company were not returned. By her first anniversary in May, a desperate Maureen asked Ray to call, too. Finally, the owner promised the albums would be ready by June 18. On June 19, Maureen was again told her photos weren't ready.

The long-awaited albums finally arrived on Friday the 13th, in July. The couple received two bride-and-groom albums and a parents' album, with an extra free album because they were unhappy with the photographer. But the couple had to send back the parents' album because the date on the cover was incorrect and a picture was damaged. By September of that year, it had not yet been returned. Once again, Maureen is calling the company weekly and has contacted the Better Business Bureau.

❤ ❤ ❤

Just as the bride and groom emerged from their hotel to have some pictures taken outdoors in New York City, a Greek Day parade passed by, blocking the street. The clever photographer took advantage of the situation by helping the bride and groom onto a passing float and following them in the parade, snapping away as they waved to the crowd. It was very picturesque—until the police stepped in and asked the bride and groom to please step down.

❤ ❤ ❤

Edna and Gene were a perfect match—a pair of real jokers. The popular couple opted to have a large wedding party—thirteen attendants on each side—all of whom were now gathered outside the California church for formal pictures before the guests' arrival.

The photographer finished shooting the bridesmaids on the church lawn and was ready to shoot the groomsmen's lineup. The best man took her aside and announced that the groomsmen had something special planned for one of the photos—would she mind?

"Of course not," replied the photographer, thinking she had seen it all. She was not prepared, however, to see the entire row of groomsmen turn their backs, drop their trousers, and moon the camera!

After that, she was ready for anything—and she got it. When the bride showed her garter, it was imprinted with one word: RUDE!

❤ ❤ ❤

Cynthia and her fiancé, Tommy, had their hearts set on a wedding in Las Vegas. The bride's family was looking forward to the weekend jaunt in the high-rolling city and made their travel reservations. Tommy's mother, however, announced that she would not travel so far from her home.

To solve the dilemma, the couple decided to secretly get married twice. The first wedding took place in the trailer court on the West Coast where the groom's mother lives. His father volunteered to tape the festivities with his new video camera, but he confused the on and off switch. "In the tape, you'd see the camera move up and point at me and Tommy, out of focus, about to take our vows," says Cynthia, laughing. "Then, the picture would move back into focus and, at the crucial moment, everything would go black—until the next shot of the ground, the inside of the trailer, or, most often, someone's feet."

The second wedding took place in a typical Las Vegas wedding chapel, before an officiant wearing a too-tight suit and a hairpiece resembling a roast. Cynthia's family members were eager to have the ceremony over and done with so that they could get back to the slot machines.

♥ ♥ ♥

Brad's teenage brother, Gary, had a passion for taking pictures. Everyone kept warning him to stay out of the professional photographer's way during the wedding, but he persisted in snapping away.

Several weeks after their elegant hotel wedding in Washington, D.C., Brad and his new wife, Gwen, got the kind of news all newly married couples dread: The professional photographer called to tell them that *none* of their wedding pictures had turned out.

All of a sudden, Gary's presence didn't seem like such a nuisance. Actually, his amateur photos—now the only record of Brad and Gwen's wedding—were quite good. So good, in fact, that they launched him on his professional career. Today, Gary is a wedding photographer in New York City.

❤ WEDDING FROM HELL NO. 7 ❤

Rebecca almost postponed her wedding when her father was unexpectedly rushed to the hospital for cataract surgery. But her father was adamant; he would walk his daughter down the aisle on the appointed day—no matter what.

As it turned out, he was prescient. Just as she and Michael had completed their plans for a wedding, the groom's briefcase, containing their wedding files, was stolen from her car. The name and address of every guest, every receipt (for rings, flowers, transportation, etc.), all the contracts for the reception hall and temple, and all the cash they had planned to use for deposits on wedding services was gone.

Since the couple were able to duplicate everything but the money, they thought things would get back to normal. Then the sky fell in—or, to put it more accurately, the bathroom ceiling. Water flooded through most of their apartment, ruining nearly all their possessions and many more important papers, and leaving them temporarily homeless.

Were three strikes enough to daunt them? Never. Rebecca and Michael simply moved in with various family members and friends, finished their arrangements, and married on their chosen date . . . secure that they could handle any curveballs life might throw them in the future.

CHAPTER 8

Lost on the Freeway of Love

♥ ♥ ♥

Even if it's just a business trip or a long
drive in the country, traveling with someone you love is wonderful. You feel close
(after all, it *is* just the two of you) and
excited, seeing new things together. But a
honeymoon should be more than just wonderful. It should be sexy and sensual. It
should make you feel extra, extra special.
It should be the most beautiful trip of your
lives.

—From *BRIDE'S Honeymoon Travel Guide*

♥ ♥ ♥

Car 54, Where Are You?

Deborah and her bridesmaids had about a half hour before they were due at the Massachusetts church. The bride had a case of butterflies, so the limousine driver stopped at a deli and went inside to buy some ginger ale while the women relaxed in the car.

Suddenly, a man who had robbed a nearby tailor's store jumped into the driver's seat and drove the limousine away! Hijacked, the women screamed at the driver until he agreed to drop them off at the church. They arrived on time—but before the uninvited chauffeur was able to pull away from the curb, Deborah's maid of honor got a parting shot. "Smile!" she called as she clicked her camera shutter. The photograph she took led to the hijacker's arrest three days later.

❤ ❤ ❤

Before Leslie's spring wedding to Doug in Massachusetts, four limousines arrived at her house: a white car for the bride, two silver limousines for the bridal party . . . and a hearse for the bride's parents.

No, it really wasn't a hearse, but the big black limo

221

looked an awful lot like one. The car company had *really* sent the wrong car.

Convinced that the hearse-like limo was bad luck, the bride refused to let members of the family step into it. Everyone proceeded to the church in the other cars. But the driver of the somber car was not to be ignored—he trailed the caravan of cars to the church, strode down the center aisle, stormed into the groom's waiting room, and demanded to be paid.

Despite being formally attired, Doug calmly told him that if he didn't leave immediately, he would "kick his butt." The driver of the limo quickly backed out of the room and left, but not before the entire front of the church had overheard the preceremony drama.

❤ ❤ ❤

A luxury limousine service that takes pride in its fleet made sure the leather interiors of the cars were cleaned and shined each week. Just how shiny were they? Well, as a wedding party was being chauffeured to a Friday evening wedding in New York, the driver hit the brakes to avoid a swerving car. As he stopped short, the entire wedding party slid off the seats and landed in a formally dressed heap on the car floor.

❤ ❤ ❤

April, who lived near the Washington church where she was to be married, realized one hour before the wedding that she'd forgotten something. No problem, she thought, I'll zip home and pick it up. She and the maid of honor ran out to the church parking lot, got in the car, and raced out onto the road.

They hadn't gone too far when April saw a truck about to make a turn from a cross street. The bride gunned the motor to beat it down the road, only to crash into a ditch beside the road. The car was seriously damaged and had to be towed, but the bride suffered only a cut on her forehead and a bruised arm.

Once traumatized family and friends were assured she was all right, the ceremony began an hour late, the bride sporting a rather rakish bandage over her left eye.

❤ ❤ ❤

It was a scene reminiscent of the ending of *The Wizard of Oz*. Allison and Brad decided to sail off to their August reception in Alaska, in a hot air balloon. But a sudden strong wind from the north carried the happy couple, maid of honor, and best man miles off course, leaving two hundred guests and parents at the reception site—a rustic lodge overlooking the ocean—waiting and worrying.

Four hours behind schedule, the newlyweds descended. They found only the remnants of a reception. Ten family members were left to greet them. Everyone else had gone home, after overcoming their anxiety long enough to plow through the buffet, the champagne, and all but one tier of the wedding cake.

Allison and Brad managed to take it in stride and dined on fresh champagne provided by the lodge owner and burgers and fries rustled up by the one remaining member of the kitchen staff. The two even had their first dance—to "Up, Up and Away!"

❤ ❤ ❤

More than one hundred guests were assembled in the twelfth-floor penthouse suite of a New Jersey hotel. Holly, the bride, left her dressing room and stepped into an elevator for her grand ascent.

But the elevator had other ideas. It stopped dead between the fifth and sixth floors. Maintenance men pried open the doors on the sixth floor, jumped on top of the cab, and manually lowered it to the basement. The now hysterical bride was informed that she would have to walk up twelve flights to her wedding because none of the elevators were working.

The bride rose to the occasion. She climbed each flight of stairs, holding her skirt and train high to keep them clean, while the wedding consultant trudged up beside her, giving a nonstop pep talk. Breathless and flushed (but quite attractively so), Holly reached the top to the applause of family and friends, and her groom, Brad—only one half hour late.

❤ ❤ ❤

A Hollywood quiz-show host and his wife planned a magnificent wedding for his daughter on a California ranch, complete with llamas, deer, and cattle. The ceremony was scheduled to begin exactly at sunset, for optimal effect, and buses had been hired to pick up guests at their hotels and shuttle them ranchward.

The buses never showed. Guests waited and waited at their assigned meeting places. Friends and relatives who had flown hundreds of miles to attend the affair finally resorted to jumping in taxis, eventually reaching the wedding site.

All of the guests finally made it. However, since the wedding had been held up for all of the late arrivals, the ceremony took place after sunset. (Because the hosts were unprepared for this later hour, there was no outdoor lighting.) As the father of the bride escorted his daughter down the now-darkened aisle, he jokingly whispered, "Anybody see a bus? Anybody see a bus?"

❤ ❤ ❤

Gail and Bob had planned a fun-filled Long Weekend Wedding for their out-of-town guests, who were all staying at a hotel in Michigan. The ceremony would be on Saturday morning, followed by the reception back at the hotel, then a postwedding brunch on Sunday morning.

The wedding consultant had hired a limousine to transport the bride and close family members to the ceremony; a bus would carry the rest of the guests. The limo was right on time, but the bus had yet to arrive. The limousine driver assured the consultant that the bus would be along any minute, but after fifteen precious minutes, the consultant sent the grandparents and an aunt and uncle off in a cab.

During the next twenty minutes, she called the limousine company three times and was reassured that the bus driver had received her letter of instructions and directions and would absolutely be there. When the consultant knew it would be a catastrophe to wait any longer, she asked the hotel doorman to hail cabs from the fleet outside the hotel. Guests were ushered into the cars four by four and given twenty-dollar bills to cover each fare.

Only when the guests began to arrive at the church did they understand what had happened to their phantom bus. The driver had been instructed by the limousine company to "just follow the limo driver," and he had taken those directions to heart. Waiting first in the hotel driveway, out of sight of the hotel, he had literally followed the limousine when it left with the bride, without loading any passengers. The bus then sat in front of the synagogue—empty.

❤ ❤ ❤

Jane was marrying Gary on a grand old yacht rented especially for the occasion. Such a ceremony demanded an equally tony readying area, so the couple had booked rooms at a grand hotel whose deluxe amenities included transportation provided by a white Rolls-Royce.

In her mind's eye Jane saw it all: the gleaming Rolls pulling up at the California pier, the bride descending as if from a cloud, a vision in white. She could just hear the jaws dropping.

The plan was for Jane to arrive in the Rolls just as the boat was scheduled to weigh anchor. The wedding consultant advised against cutting her arrival so close to the ceremony, but the bride was adamant. Be deprived of a grand entrance? Never.

But as soon as she checked into the hotel, things started going wrong. Jane asked for her luggage. It was nowhere to be found (later she found out that Gary, who had already left for the ceremony, had checked in her baggage under his name). When she finally got her luggage, she couldn't remember "the safe place" where she had packed her mother's heirloom pearls. And when she was finally dressed (pearls and all), and settled into her Rolls-Royce, the luxury car became ignominiously stuck in a traffic jam.

Rather than make a grand entrance, Jane arrived at her own wedding one-and-a-half hours late. The reception had to be shortened to two-and-a-half hours because the boat had been chartered for a specific amount of time and was scheduled to sail for another party later that evening.

But while Jane regarded the event as something of a disaster, her guests had a great time. When it became apparent that the bride had been mysteriously delayed (there was no phone on the boat for her to call, after all), the wedding consultant simply started serving cocktails. By the time Jane showed up, a sense of catastrophe was the farthest thing from anyone's mind.

❤ ❤ ❤

Everything went as planned on the spring wedding day of Cheryl and Max, with one exception: the limousine forgot to pick up the bride at her Minnesota hotel.

While all the guests waited—and wondered—if she was going to show up, Cheryl paced the hotel lobby in her wedding gown, as a group of foreign tourists took pictures of her. Fortunately, a family friend staying at the hotel was also running late. He had hired his own limo, and as soon as he spotted Cheryl, he offered her his car.

Among the couple's most prized wedding checks: the refund from the limousine company.

❤ ❤ ❤

For their Texas spring wedding Kim and Greg arranged for a limousine service to take all of the out-of-town guests—including Greg's parents—from the Midwest hotel to the church.

The limo arrived on schedule, but Greg's mother insisted that it was far too early to depart—besides, the ceremony was just three miles away. Sending her husband on ahead of her, she went to the hotel beauty salon to have her hair styled. Once suitably coiffed for her son's wedding, she hailed a cab to the church.

One hour and $67.50 later, she finally arrived at the church forty miles away. She quickly realized the error, and with more than a few hairs now out of place, she rushed back into the cab and demanded to be taken to the right church. Then she slammed the cab door on her pale peach chiffon gown.

One hour later, the mother of the groom finally arrived. The minister thanked the cab company for finally bringing them all together, and a hastily arranged hand-tied bouquet concealed the ugly black oil streak on her dress quite nicely.

❤ ❤ ❤

On the way to Betty and Tim's fall wedding in Connecticut, guests were amused when they passed an unusual convoy. Parked by the side of the road were a horse-drawn carriage and two antique cars hired by the bride and groom to transport them and their attendants to the ceremony. The vintage vehicles had mistakenly parked at a site nearly three miles from the church.

Close friends spotted the convoy and pointed it in the right direction. It arrived at the church thirty minutes late, just as guests were wondering whether the couple had had second thoughts.

❤ ❤ ❤

Samantha and Dan were holding their wedding reception some distance down the freeway from where they were married in California. It seemed like everyone had found the place with no trouble, so the bride and groom began assembling a receiving line.

Then Dan realized his parents were nowhere to be found. And no one could remember having seen them leave the church. Dan began to panic. His parents were elderly, they were from out-of-town, and they were in a rental car.

Frantic phone calls were made to the church, local hospitals, other inns in the area with similar names, and the police—all to no avail.

Samantha and Dan wouldn't think of proceeding without them, so they sat down to wait. And wait. And wait.

Finally, after an hour or so, Dan's parents came rolling in, a trifle bedraggled but none the worse for wear. It turned out that they had missed their freeway exit and had to travel miles out of the way to reach the next one and turn around.

The first song the DJ played? "Freeway of Love"!

❤ ❤ ❤

While driving in their rented limousine from the ceremony to the reception, California newlyweds Paula and Peter spotted a familiar-looking car ahead of them. It was Peter's car—stolen two days before the wedding!

The bride and groom did what any self-respecting newlyweds would do—they ordered the limo driver to give chase, and eventually forced the car to pull over. The formally dressed couple then made a citizen's arrest, with the excited bride giving one of the "alleged thieves" a bop on the head with her large bouquet for good measure. Alerted by passersby, the police arrived and placed the two men (who claimed they had just bought the car and were unaware that it was stolen) under arrest.

Honeymoon Horrors

Melanie and Mike's honeymoon would have fit nicely on a double bill with *Creature From the Black Lagoon*.

The couple decided to explore an unpopulated island within sight of Tahiti, their honeymoon destination. Although the hotel staff were willing to take them over by boat for an afternoon visit, they tried to discourage the romantic overnight stay that the couple had in mind. It would be such a memorable night, they thought, sleeping alone on the beach of their "own" island under a starlit sky.

The couple convinced the skipper of a motorboat to leave them on the island with their blankets and picnic basket, and arranged for him to return to pick them up the next morning. Reluctantly, the skipper departed in the late afternoon, still urging them to accompany him back to Tahiti. They refused, and waved him off confidently.

It was so romantic—sitting on the deserted island, watching the most perfect sunset they'd ever seen. And then, to their horror, in the approaching dusk, they watched two, then dozens, and then hundreds of land crabs start to hoist themselves ashore for the night. They were trapped! With each step away from the shoreline, the crabs followed. It became apparent that the crustaceans intended to inhabit every square inch of land.

Terrified—and disgusted—the couple managed to climb a tree, which is where the native boat skipper found them the next morning when he returned. "So much for romance," says Jane. "We were both sore for days from sitting in that tree!"

❤ ❤ ❤

Sam and Helen planned to leave for their Florida honeymoon right after their hotel wedding on the West Side of Manhattan. The bride's complete trousseau was stashed in the trunk, leaving the backseat of the car for the very tall groom's wardrobe—shirts, pants, shorts, and robe (all painstakingly special-ordered by his mother).

When the couple emerged after the festivities in their going-away outfits, they were distraught to find out that the car, which had been parked on the street, had been broken into. All of the groom's clothes were gone, leaving him with only the jeans and shirt he was wearing for the two-week trip. The couple called their insurance company and then decided to look on the bright side—at least they had a valid excuse for a honeymoon spending spree.

❤ ❤ ❤

By the time Barb and Bill got up to their room in the hotel that had hosted their reception, it was two-thirty a.m. Forget about romance—they fell exhausted into bed, hoping to catch at least forty winks before getting up and catching an early-morning plane to London.

When they woke up a few hours later, they discovered there was no hot water in the hotel. They were grubby enough from eight hours of stress and dancing, "But even worse," recalls Barb, "my dress was so heavy and the bodice was so tightly boned that I had covered myself with back ointment before going to bed. I reeked of Ben-Gay!"

Fate intervened, however—they had an empty seat between them for the long journey.

❤ ❤ ❤

The temperature was just under 100 degrees on the summer night that Arthur and Diane checked into their honeymoon hotel. Inside their room, it must have been close to 120 degrees. They looked along all of the walls, but couldn't find a switch to turn on the air-conditioning and were to embarrassed to call the front desk.

Diane begged her new husband to at least open the window. But he had just seen the movie *Psycho* for the first time. What if someone slipped in through the window and attacked them while they slept? he asked seriously.

The two got into bed and spent a fitful night tossing and turning, dripping in sweat. Romance? No way—they could hardly breathe.

Diane finally got out of bed at six a.m. While Arthur was still asleep, she decided to open the window.

He'd never know the difference, she reasoned. There, on the windowsill, were the controls to the air-conditioner.

WEDDING PORTRAIT
Dick Rodgers' Rocky Honeymoon Cruise

❤ ❤ ❤

On March 5, 1930, composer Dick Rodgers and his wife, Dorothy, were married after a courtship that began aboard an ocean liner and culminated in a ceremony in her parents' living room on Park Avenue in New York City.

Considering how the couple had met, it seemed only fitting that their honeymoon be aboard a ship—the U.S.S. *Roma*. About ten days into their trip, the peaceful sea calm was shattered. Dorothy was awakened at five a.m. by Dick's painful moans. He was convinced that he was having an appendicitis attack. An operation wasn't necessary; they spent two days ashore in a monastery in Taormina, where with ministrations from the monks and his new wife, he recuperated enough to continue the wedding trip.

❤ ❤ ❤

Susie and Bob couldn't believe their good fortune when Susie's aunt and uncle invited them to use their cabin during their honeymoon. After their colonial-style wedding in New England, the couple were looking forward to a week of isolated romantic bliss.

On their wedding night, they were touched when they arrived to find all of the lights on and a fire burning in the fireplace. "How thoughtful of them to leave everything ready for us," commented Susie as they took their bags out of the car. Imagine their surprise, though, when Bob carried Susie over the threshold and almost dumped her into the welcoming, outspread arms of her uncle. Her aunt emerged from the kitchen right behind him to officially welcome them to their home, as guests—for the next week!

"They were incredibly discreet, and tried to give us some privacy, but they really intended to stay there with us the entire honeymoon," sighed Susie. "We stayed a few days, then made a tactful excuse and drove on to another location—on our own."

❤ ❤ ❤

John thought he had packed exceptionally well for the European jaunt that he and Maude had planned for their July wedding. They were at the airport right on time for their seven p.m. flight to Paris, excited about the two weeks ahead.

While standing in line to check in, John realized that

he couldn't find his passport. Although Maude desperately rifled through his carryon bag, John knew that he had left it in his apartment, on the mail table near the door, for safekeeping. In the rush of leaving for the wedding, he had picked up his luggage, grabbed the ticket envelope, but left the passport behind.

None of the friends or relatives who had a key to John's apartment were home yet to answer the phone. The flights and hotel had been paid in advance, and it was difficult to reschedule flights because it was the tourist season. John convinced Maude to fly to Paris on her own, resigned that they'd spend their first married nights apart.

The next day, John returned to the airport with his passport. Taking pity on him, the airline put him at the top of the standby list. With the time change working in his favor, John was able to join his bride on the third morning of their honeymoon.

❤ ❤ ❤

After their morning wedding and reception, Eliza and Stuart flew to New York City where they would spend their wedding night before flying on to their honeymoon destination. Thinking that the occasion demanded a romantic view, they had booked what the hotel dubbed the Penthouse Suite.

After checking in, Eliza and Stuart were taken by the bellboy via a special elevator to the top floor. He then led them up a spiral staircase to their suite. As promised, the view was stupendous—but the sleeping arrangements were not at all what the newlyweds had in mind.

"We can't spend our wedding night in twin beds!" they complained to the manager.

"No problem," said the manager. "We'll send someone from housekeeping to investigate."

Eliza and Stuart sat on their twin beds and waited for housekeeping. After half an hour passed, they phoned again.

"No problem," said the housekeeping representative who arrived eventually. "You can push the twin beds together and we'll just bring up a double-bed mattress to lay on top."

Eliza and Stuart pushed the beds together as instructed and waited for the double mattress to be sent up. After yet another long interval, a great commotion was heard at the front of the spiral staircase.

It was the maintenance men with the double-bed mattress. Try as they might, the mattress could not be maneuvered upward.

Giving up, the couple asked for another room. "We have a problem," responded the manager. "We are totally booked."

It was up to the bride and groom to be resourceful. They turned the two twin-bed mattresses horizontally across the pushed-together beds, and did their best to enjoy the starlight view.

❤ ❤ ❤

When Arthur and Amy booked passages on their honeymoon cruise, they thought they had found the quintessential setting for romance. They neglected to inquire

WEDDING PORTRAIT
Mayor Diane Feinstein's Major Slipup

❤ ❤ ❤

Diane Feinstein, then mayor of San Francisco, and her fiancé, Richard Blum, had planned a European honeymoon after their wedding on January 20, 1980. But plans called for a stop in Washington, D.C., to meet with Vice President Mondale. Unfortunately, an unexpected occurrence put a crimp in her plans. Ms. Feinstein fell in the White House driveway, fractured her arm, and spent her honeymoon wearing a sling.

about the ages of the other passengers on board, however, and by the time they set sail they had discovered that their shipmates were largely senior citizens who preferred music from the forties, shuffleboard, and afternoon tea.

At first disappointed, the couple then vowed to be hardy sailors. They allowed the elders to pamper them at meals, answered their numerous, good-natured questions politely, and spent a good part of their crossing of the Atlantic holed up in their cabin with buckets of champagne.

❤ ❤ ❤

While driving home from the reception (still garbed in tuxedo and wedding dress), Paul and Jenny, both of New York City, were set upon by four men in ski masks who forced them from their car at gunpoint. After throwing the bride to the pavement, the thieves made off with the car and approximately thirteen thousand dollars worth of cash and gifts, including the top of the wedding cake (saved for good luck) and other reception favors.

But love conquers all—especially when a honeymoon beckons. The next morning, the couple departed for their Caribbean cruise—the one gift from their wedding that the thieves would not be enjoying.

Acknowledgments

BRIDE'S especially thanks Managing Editor Andrea Feld for ensuring that Wedding Nightmares became a dream come true. Thanks, too, to former staff member Julia Martin, who launched the "Wedding Nightmares" column in BRIDE'S, and to writer Libby Morse for finessing the writing style of the final manuscript. A further note of gratitude to Tracy Gill for expert reporting, to Kathy Mullins for research on historical wedding nightmares, and to reporters Miriam Arond, Diane Botnick, and Amy Krieger Rippis. Thanks, also to BRIDE'S staff members Wendy Caisse Curran, Heather Twidale, Paula Derrow, Sue Bruskin, Julia Califano, Wendy Marder, and former staff member Robyn Liverant for their reporting and help in manuscript preparation—and to BRIDE'S Travel Editor Sally Kilbridge, for sharing honeymoon nightmares heard along the way. Inside illustrations were conceptualized by BRIDE'S Art Director, Phyllis Richmond Cox.

BRIDE'S also thanks its many readers and friends who related their personal tales of wedding woe; all names have been changed. Hats off, as well, to the following wedding professionals nationwide who shared humorous and disastrous experiences observed over the years:

Bakers/Caterers—Linda Abbey, Great Performances, New York, New York; Anthony Cornelia, general manager, Huntington Townhouse, Huntington Station, New York; Tracy Davis, Party Artistry, New York, New York; Florence Dziuk, Cakes and Catering Exceptionale, Inc., Minneapolis, Minnesota; Mark Fahrer, Caterer, New York, New York; Ilda Gale, Cuisine, Cuisine II, Port Washington, New York; Mark Levenstein, co-owner of Levenstein and Sarnoff Caterers, Lawrence, New York; Maureen Murphy, former banquet manager, The Grand Prospect Hall, Brooklyn, New York; Barry Ress, The Crystal Plaza, Livingston, New Jersey; Robert Zweben, The Shadowbrook, Shrewsbury, New Jersey.

Bridal-salon owners—Renée Strauss, Renée Strauss for the Bride, Beverly Hills, California.

Limousine Companies—Carole Bagnasco, D & E Limousine Service, Deer Park, New York.

Musicians—Retired organist Elizabeth Silance Ballard, Chesapeake, Virginia; bandleader Bill Conway, Swing Express, Astoria, New York; Robert Fazio, Music Man Productions, North Babylon, New York; Cynthia Bolgrad Goldman, The Music Mistress, Ridgewood, New Jersey; Joseph Guadagne and Nick Jordan, Nick Jordon Orchestras—Music Makers DJs, San Francisco, California; Hank Lane, Hank Lane Music, Great Neck, New York; Danny Petrow, The Danny Petrow Band, New York, New York; Joe Rondi, D-Jay Joey & Company,

Lynbrook, New York; Andy Zoob, Zoob Orchestra, New York, New York.

Officiants—The Honorable Buck Allen, municipal court judge, Vail, Colorado; Father Albert E. Amend, St. Andrew's Episcopal Church, Williston Park, New York; Father Tim Brown, Loyola College, Baltimore, Maryland; The Reverend Edward J. Wright, Corte Madera, California.

Photographers/Videographers—Susan Frank, San Francisco, California; Terry deRoy Gruber, New York, New York; Bill Hamm, Bill's Valuable Videos, San Anselmo, California; Ben Janken, San Francisco, California; Fred Marcus and Andrew Marcus, Fred Marcus Photography Studio, New York, New York.

Wedding Consultants—John Arguelles, formerly of California Celebrations, Marina del Rey, California; Ann Axelrod, Port Washington, New York; Regan Botts-Washington, Melange Wedding Coordinators, Arlington, Virginia; Elza Burton, Your Special Day, Mill Valley, California; Cindy Cerretta, former office manager, White Glove Affairs, Eastchester, New York; Colin Cowie, Los Angeles, California; Roxanne Davis, Accents, Conroe, Texas; Mary Dreyhaupt, Islip, New York; Robbi Ernst, III, June Wedding, Inc., San Francisco, California; Frank Foust, Down the Aisle, Anchorage, Alaska; Joan Freese, Event Resource & Design, San Rafael, California; Kelly Gladder and Annena Sorenson, Tie the Knot Wedding Consultants, San Francisco, California; Ginger Grantham, The Bridal Patch, Hanceville, Alabama; Lynn Jeter, Lynn Allen Jeter & Associates,

Beverly Hills, California; Gayle Labenow, You Are Cordially Invited, Babylon, New York; Cynthia Leggiere, Your Perfect Wedding, Bayshore, New York; Shirley Locke, Huntington Woods, Michigan; Ella Mae Malec, Malec's Wedding Service, South Bend, Indiana; Yvonne McClendon, The Bride's Day, Detroit, Michigan; Allison O'Neal, Weddings Northwest, Redmond, Washington; Mary Park, Mary Park Unlimited, Inc., Culver City, California; Lois Pearce, Beautiful Occasions, Inc., Hamden, Connecticut; Shirley Richie, SSR Enterprises, Washington, D.C.; Elizabeth May Sanders, Interior Accents, Highland Park, New Jersey; Domenic Santana, Celebrations of New York & New Jersey, Jersey City, New Jersey; Alice Small, Houston, Texas; Rita Bloom Smith, Bethesda, Maryland; Mary C. Weaver, Farmington, Connecticut.